Partisanship

Other Books in the At Issue Series

COVID-19 and Other Pandemics
Food Security
Genocide
Is America a Democracy or an Oligarchy?
The Media's Influence on Society
Money Laundering
Nuclear Anxiety
Open Borders
Policing in America
The Politicization of the Supreme Court

Partisanship

Carla Mooney, Book Editor

Published in 2022 by Greenhaven Publishing, LLC
353 3rd Avenue, Suite 255, New York, NY 10010

First Edition

Articles in Greenhaven Publishing anthologies are often edited for length to meet page requirements. In addition, original titles of these works are changed to clearly present the main thesis and to explicitly indicate the author's opinion. Every effort is made to ensure that Greenhaven Publishing accurately reflects the original intent of the authors. Every effort has been made to trace the owners of the copyrighted material.

Cover image: Rawpixel.com/Shutterstock

Library of Congress Cataloging-in-Publication Data

Names: Mooney, Carla, 1970- editor.
Title: Partisanship / Carla Mooney, book editor.
Description: First edition. | New York : Greenhaven Publishing, 2022. | Series: At issue | Includes bibliographical references and index. | Audience: Ages 15+ | Audience: Grades 10–12 | Summary: "Anthology of diverse perspectives that examine what partisanship means today, how this differs from historical partisanship, its contributing factors, and the effect it has on the United States."—Provided by publisher.
Identifiers: LCCN 2020050959 | ISBN 9781534508170 (library binding) | ISBN 9781534508163 (paperback) | ISBN 9781534508187 (ebook)
Subjects: LCSH: Political culture—United States—Juvenile literature. | Partisanship—United States—Juvenile literature.
Classification: LCC JK1726 .P3585 2022 | DDC 306.20973—dc23
LC record available at https://lccn.loc.gov/2020050959

Manufactured in the United States of America

Website: http://greenhavenpublishing.com

Contents

Introduction

In an era of increasing partisanship, the divide between America's political parties appears greater than ever. Distrust, hostility, and anger have become more common in politics than handshakes and compromise.

In exploring partisanship, one must consider how partisanship develops and also its effect on American democracy. Does some level of partisanship enrich American democracy and make it stronger? Or does partisanship hinder democracy's ability to function effectively? At some point, does partisanship become so obstructive that it blocks the government's ability to pass legislation supported by the majority of citizens and effectively perform fundamental governmental duties?

Throughout America's political history, the country has experienced fluctuating levels of bipartisan compromise and polarizing partisanship. In the years before the Civil War, disagreements between political parties incited violence in Congress on numerous occasions, according to historian Joanne Freeman in her 2018 book, *The Field of Blood: Violence in Congress and the Road to Civil War*. In 1838, partisan rancor led Representative William Graves of Kentucky to challenge Representative Jonathan Cilley of Maine to a duel over an insult to his character, which led to Cilley's death.

While physical fights diminished in the 20th century, partisan conflict rose and fell. During the decades from the 1930s into the 1970s, a bipartisan compromise emerged as a coalition of Republicans and Southern Democrats worked together to achieve common goals. Although partisanship began to rise again in the 1980s, political parties were still able to find some areas of common ground. For example, in 1990, Republican and Democratic members of Congress worked together to pass the bipartisan Americans with Disabilities Act, making it against the law to discriminate based on disability. And in 2012, Congress passed bipartisan legislation known as the Jumpstart Our Business Startups (JOBS) Act, designed to help entrepreneurs and small businesses. In a statement at the time, former House majority leader Eric Cantor said, "The bipartisan JOBS Act represents an increasingly rare legislative victory in Washington where both sides seized the opportunity to work together, improved the bill, and passed it with strong bipartisan support."

Although there are examples of bipartisan compromise in American history, some commentators point out that this was not the intent of the country's Founding Fathers. In a February 2020 article published on Time.com, Fergus M. Bordewich, the author of *Congress at War: How Republican Reformers Fought the Civil War, Defied Lincoln, Ended Slavery, and Remade America*, writes, "The low esteem in which Congress is held today may well be more rooted in a widespread but false idea that government is supposed to be smooth, efficient, and collaborative, and that compromises are easy. None of that is true. The Founders knew from the beginning that republican politics would be messy and full of conflict. In fact, they were proud of it, because they recognized it as democracy in action." Even though bipartisanship has led to compromise legislation, some writers argue that excessive bipartisanship harms democracy. According to this viewpoint, when politicians reach across the aisle to work with their opposition counterparts, it becomes more difficult for voting citizens to hold them accountable in elections. In this way, partisanship improves American democracy and allows it to function most effectively.

Yet other writers contend that while partisanship may give voters clear choices in elections, excessive partisanship prevents the US government from working efficiently. They point out that partisan fights lead to legislative priorities becoming mired in political gridlock. When partisanship dominates the political arena, politicians may be more likely to support or oppose policies and programs based on which party proposed it, not on the policy or program's individual merits or its benefits for constituents.

In an article for the *Washington Post* published in January 2014, Sarah Binder, a professor of political science at George Washington University and a senior fellow at the Brookings Institution, writes that "our political system requires broad, usually bipartisan, coalitions to adopt major policy change. Such coalitions are easier to build when a sufficient mass of legislators occupy the political center to bridge partisan and ideological divisions."

Some observers warn that rising partisanship has the potential to do tremendous harm to democracy. Partisanship divides citizens into political sides. As each side becomes more polarized, the divide between the opposing parties grows wider while shared political ground and objectives shrink. In the 2019 book *Democracies Divided: The Global Challenge of Political Polarization*, Thomas Carothers and Andrew O'Donohue of the Brookings Institution warn of the dangers of partisanship: "It routinely weakens respect for democratic norms, corrodes basic legislative processes, undermines the nonpartisan stature of the judiciary, and fuels public disaffection with political parties. It exacerbates intolerance and discrimination, diminishes societal trust, and increases violence throughout the society. Moreover, it reinforces and entrenches itself, dragging countries into a downward spiral of anger and division for which there are no easy remedies."

Some political commentators point out that the recent rise in partisanship has been driven by more than policy disagreements. Political parties are increasingly being defined by ideology, race, religion, and geography. These characteristics are at the core of each group's identity and make it easier to see the opposing party members as the enemy. From this viewpoint, it becomes easier to dehumanize the other side. Rather than coming together to solve problems and achieve common goals, partisans care more about beating the other side. Alan Abramowitz, a professor of political science at Emory University, and graduate student Steven Webster write in a 2017 Politico article that "over the past few decades, American politics has become like a bitter sports rivalry, in which the parties hang together mainly out of sheer hatred of the other team, rather than a shared sense of purpose."

The viewpoints in *At Issue: Partisanship* offer differing perspectives on partisanship and its role in American democracy. Some writers emphasize the benefits of partisanship and how it can strengthen democratic debate, policy making, and elections. Others highlight the harmful effects of partisanship and the repercussions it has on society as a whole. A discussion of the role of partisanship in a democracy is one that requires careful examination of the sources, nature, and scope of partisanship in American politics today to understand best its potential effects in the years to come.

1

Excessive Bipartisanship Is a Historical Problem

Sam Rosenfeld

Sam Rosenfeld is an assistant professor of political science at Colgate University. His research focuses on political parties and American political development.

In the mid-1900s, observers viewed excessive bipartisanship and compromise as a central problem in US politics. They argued that bipartisan lawmaking made it difficult for voters to hold political parties accountable in elections. Reformers on the left and right called for political parties organized around distinct ideologies and policy positions. They believed America would benefit from a more partisan political system. By the 1980s, partisanship in US politics resurged. However, party reformers may have underestimated the bitter hostility and rancor of party polarization and the governmental dysfunctions that occur in a more partisan political system.

Everyone says they hate partisanship and political attacks. As a recent Pew survey showed, large majorities of Americans recognize that current politics are marked by discord and believe that it is important for Democrats and Republicans to work together on issues and for the tone of political debate to be respectful. Scholarly and popular books proliferate—to diagnose the pathologies of partisanship, blame them for governmental

"What History Teaches About Partisanship and Polarization," by Sam Rosenfeld, Scholars Strategy Network, July 23, 2018. Reprinted by permission.

dysfunction, and even suggest that partisan polarization is undermining democracy itself.

Angst over contemporary hyper-partisanship easily turns into nostalgia for a bygone era of comity and compromise. But this obscures a complicated, and ironic, history. As my new book *The Polarizers* details, more than half a century ago, leading scholars, journalists, and politicians also decried dysfunctions and called for reforms. But ironically those observers identified excessive bipartisanship as the central problem in US politics, and called for more polarization. This past debate matters, because understanding problems in the earlier, less partisan-polarized era of mid-twentieth century US politics and the calls of critics for more partisanship can help Americans today better address contemporary democratic dilemmas.

When Bipartisanship Was the Problem

The mid-twentieth century was a period marked by unique levels of bipartisanship in US lawmaking. Although often attributed to an overarching postwar "consensus," such cross-party collaboration is more accurately seen as a byproduct of the huge ideological range contained within the ranks of each of the two overlapping major parties. Because key ideological divides of the period cross-cut rather than reinforced the partisan divide, most lawmaking was carried out via bipartisan coalitions. And congressional deals were forged by powerful committee chairs who were granted key decentralized authority by party leaders. Thanks to seniority rules, those committee chairs were disproportionately longtime incumbents from the uncompetitive one-party South. Norms of civility and across-the-aisle camaraderie made sense in such a system. "Integrity crosses party lines," a Republican told one scholar analyzing Senate mores in the 1950s. "You rely on some of your Democratic colleagues equally."

This mid-century cross-partisan system was strongly criticized, however, by observers who made a democratic case against the fuzzily indistinct parties and argued that bipartisan lawmaking blurred lines of political accountability, making it difficult for voters to know which office-holders to hold responsible in elections. Reforms were pushed most forcefully by a committee of political scientists who called in 1950 for "responsible party government" run by programmatic parties organized around coherent and distinct policy positions rather than ties of tradition, patronage, or personality. They believed America would benefit from a system in which the parties "bring forth programs to which they commit themselves and ... possess sufficient internal cohesion to carry out these programs."

Architects of Party Polarization

This argument had impact. It informed the actions of activists and reformers on the left and right who worked consciously during the second half of the twentieth century to reshape the parties and their operations around internally cohesive and mutually distinct ideologies.

Early advocates for reform were liberal Democrats frustrated by the obstacles other party members posed to liberal policymaking. They found support from ideological groups, civil rights advocates, and the progressive wing of organized labor. As these activists battled the traditional political machines for state and local control of Democratic organizations in the North, they also attacked the outsized national power of segregationist southerners. Meanwhile, conservative Republicans advocated for a partisan realignment that would unite southern whites and northern Republicans. By the 1960s, Democratic-backed national responses to the civil rights movement made many southerners amenable to changes, as large numbers of northern Republican transplants were moving South and intellectuals fashioned a national conservative agenda that included opposition to aggressive federal civil rights enforcement.

A wave of institutional reforms in the 1970s provided a new environment for redrawing the lines of ideology and partisanship. Liberals pursued congressional rules changes that empowered party leaders, ended automatic seniority, and made committee chairmanships subject to the vote of the Democratic rank and file. Simultaneously, sweeping reforms of the parties' presidential nominating procedures shifted control away from party actors and toward outside groups and primary election voters. Both sets of reforms rendered the political system more permeable and responsive to ideological activism. Liberal and conservative activists alike channeled the movements and issues emerging from the tumult of the 1960s into new base party coalitions.

From the 1980s on, party adherents sorted out along ideological lines, catalyzing a partisan resurgence that has continued, unabated, into the troubled present.

Coming to Terms with Polarization

This new world seems to fulfill the vision of mid-century responsible party reformers, yet they would likely be just as dissatisfied as today's citizens. It turns out that they underestimated the virulence of party polarization in practice, which can reach toxic levels when team spirit is reinforced by shared worldviews and core social identities. They also failed to anticipate the institutional dysfunctions that would happen when disciplined, programmatic parties tried to operate within America's Madisonian constitutional system laden with "veto points." In this system, minority parliamentary-style parties have incentives to obstruct the legislative process, rather than participate in governing compromises.

The ill "fit" between polarized parties and US governing institutions may have to be rectified by institutional changes—such as getting rid of the Senate's 60-vote requirement to break a filibuster. Of course, ending filibusters is an example of a reform intended to allow partisan majorities to more easily implement their agenda when in power, a change that would accommodate rather than mitigate polarized partisanship. Most Americans resist this kind of accommodation, but the story of the postwar polarizers reveals that there are hard trade-offs between worthy goals in the US system—trade-offs between pragmatic bargaining and coherent policymaking, between clubby elite comity and democratic participation and accountability. A sense of realism about those tradeoffs may be long overdue.

2

Partisan Politics Increasingly Divides the US Electorate

Bob Abeshouse

Bob Abeshouse is a producer and reporter for People & Power, *an investigative documentary program that examines the use and abuse of power.*

Rising partisanship in the United States has divided voters into two distinct political parties defined by ideology, race, religion, and geography. Distinct social divisions make it easier for members of one political party to dehumanize the other side and see them as the enemy. In this increasingly toxic, partisan atmosphere, political parties often care more about beating the other side than working together to identify and solve community problems. This growing division and blind allegiance to a political party may threaten American democracy.

Americans may be as divided over politics today as they were in the lead up to the Civil War of the 1860s. In Washington, DC, hardly a day passes without Democrats and Republicans accusing the other party of betraying the nation and its core values. Around the country, partisan allegiances are fracturing relationships at the level of the family, neighbourhood and community. Religious congregations are coming apart over politics. So are marriages.

Republished with permission of SyndiGate Media Inc., from "The Disunited States: How Partisan Politics Is Polarising the US," by Bob Abeshouse, Al Jazeera Media Network, August 2, 2019. Permission conveyed through Copyright Clearance Center, Inc.

Partisan rancour worsened after the April release of Special Counsel Robert Mueller's report on his investigation of President Donald Trump and whether his campaign cooperated with the Russians in the 2016 presidential race. According to a recent poll, 68 percent of Republicans believe that the Mueller report cleared Trump, but only eight percent of Democrats feel the same way.

The real scandal, Republicans argue, is that the FBI spied on Trump's campaign. As Republican Senator Josh Hawley of Missouri asserted at a judiciary committee hearing, "If this can go on in the United States, we don't have a democracy any more."

For presidential candidate Senator Elizabeth Warren and other Democrats, Mueller's report documented evidence of obstruction of justice and other misdeeds by President Trump that call for impeachment hearings to begin immediately. Protecting and serving the Constitution of the United States, she says, demands nothing less.

Yet while Trump openly exacerbates the toxic partisanship and political incivility that is rampant in the US today, he is not the cause of it, according to Lilliana Mason, a professor at the University of Maryland. She argues that he has brought "into the open divides that have been accumulating between the parties" for decades.

In her recent book, *Uncivil Agreement*, Mason attributes political polarisation and extreme partisanship in the US to a social sorting process that has divided the country's electorate into two political parties defined by distinct ideological, racial, religious and geographic groups. Between the 1960s and now, "the Republican party has become largely white, Christian, rural, somewhat more male," she says. "And the Democratic party is somewhat everyone else: non-white, non-Christian, relatively urban or suburban, and more female because we have a gender gap that's been growing."

"It starts to feel like every election isn't just about our parties competing," she says. "It's about our racial groups and our religious groups and our geographical groups, and if you lose, it's not just your party that lost, it's all of the things that make up your individual identity, all the groups you feel attached to. It's almost like they all lost too."

This sorting of people into two political camps fuels stereotyping and suspicion. In a 2018 poll by Nielsen, 70 percent of Republicans and 60 percent of Democrats agreed that the opposing party was a serious threat to the United States.

Identity Politics

In the past, it was common for people with similar social characteristics to be in both parties—what political scientists call cross-cutting cleavages. It muted partisanship and had a humanising effect because there were people on the other side like you, Mason explains. But as "we become more socially distinct as partisans it's a lot easier to dehumanise the other group. And so, we start to think of the other side as not only opponents but actually enemies and dangerous."

The increasing allegiance to a party not only threatens personal relationships but democratic norms. "If you care only about whether your party wins or loses and you care about nothing else then there is no governing, there is no accountability, there is no impeachment," Mason adds. "The only thing that matters is beating the other side and being winners again."

One of the best places to investigate America's toxic divisions is North Carolina. The state has been a hotbed of partisan conflict for decades, and political warfare escalated after Republicans seized control of the state legislature in 2010.

"North Carolina is ground zero when it comes to polarisation," according to Rob Christensen, a political author and reporter who covered politics in the state for 45 years at the *Raleigh News and Observer*.

"The problem for the strategists is that the state's not one thing, it's many things. The state has a little bit of Alabama in it, state has a little bit of Silicon Valley in it, state has a little bit of Berkeley in it, the state has a little bit of Harlem in it. I mean it's a really interesting mix and a very volatile mix."

The 2020 Republican Convention will be held in North Carolina, underscoring its importance in the presidential race. "The closeness of the races means both parties think they can win," Christensen says. He points out that Barack Obama carried North Carolina in 2008 by the smallest margin of any state he won. Mitt Romney won the state in 2012, also by the smallest margin of any state he carried.

In 2016, Trump campaigned hard in North Carolina and won the state by three-and-a-half points. Part of the reason, according to Christensen, was that "Donald Trump was in part a backlash against Barack Obama. There was just total shock and unacceptance by some substantial minority of the population to see a black man as president of the United States."

In fact, in 2007, whites in the US were just as likely to identify with Democrats as Republicans, according to a Pew Research Center study. But whites fled the Democratic party during Obama's presidency. By 2016, there was a 15 percent difference between the parties. Race plays a central role in political polarisation and incivility in the US today. "Race is certainly a very, very powerful issue and we haven't yet come to grips with it," Christensen says.

"Fine People on Both Sides"

North Carolina occupies a special place in the history of civil rights in the US. In 1960, four African-American college students in Greensboro famously sat down at a "white-only" lunch counter at a Woolworths department store to order coffee. They were arrested, sparking a lunch counter sit-in that lasted for six months.

The Woolworths sit-in was a catalyst for a youth-led sit-in movement across the country that helped create momentum for the passage of the Civil Rights Act of 1964 and the 1965 Voting Rights Act. Moderate Democrats led the fight for the legislation. Their support set the stage for the racial sorting between the parties that we see today, according to Mason. "When the Democratic party chose to be the party of civil rights, that really angered a huge portion of the people who identified as Democrats, namely white southern Democrats," she says.

"It helped pull away a lot of conservative Democrats into the Republican party," Christensen says. "They started voting for people like George Wallace who was a Democrat although he ran at some point as a third-party candidate. And then essentially, they began crossing over into voting for Richard Nixon or Ronald Reagan or Donald Trump today. This has happened all across the south, dividing up along racially polarised lines, but you know that's true nationally."

A good example of this racial shift between the parties took place in Lenoir County, North Carolina. Two bloody Civil War battles were fought near Kinston, a city in the county that has a replica of a Confederate gunship in a downtown park. According to Mike Parker, the commander of the local chapter—or "camp"—of the Sons of Confederate Veterans, about two-thirds of the white voters in the county are registered as Republicans, a shift from the past. There are about 800 Sons of Confederate Veterans chapters across the American South, made up of men descended from Confederate soldiers.

"More men died in the Civil War than died in all the other wars we've ever fought put together," Parker says. "Down here it involved almost every family and this is one reason why I think in the South the Civil War is such a big deal."

Parker takes issue with the idea that racial tensions worsened because Obama was elected president. "It's too easy to just say well he was a black man therefore white people didn't like him," Parker says. "There are people who just say look, we don't want socialism, we don't want these huge government programmes." Still, Parker noted that he thought Obama "constantly seemed to me to play a race card."

Parker is a supporter of President Trump's economic policies and efforts to build a wall on the Mexico-US border. Asked about Trump's response to an August 2017 Unite the Right rally in Charlottesville, Virginia, to protest against the removal of a statue of Confederate General Robert E. Lee from a park, Parker did not express any concern about the president's comments. At a press conference, Trump equated white supremacist organisers of the rally with counter-protestors who came to confront them. Violence erupted in Charlottesville leaving 30 injured and a counter-protester dead. "I think there is blame on both sides. And I don't have any doubt about it," Trump said at the time. He added, "You also had people that were very fine people on both sides."

Parker says that Trump "wasn't talking about there being good people among the white supremacy clan." He believes the president was referring to other people like "history buffs" who came to Charlottesville to defend the monument. "I mean not everybody who thinks the monuments should stay there is a racist," he says.

"Racism Is Always in Play"

Many Democrats believe that anyone who supports Trump is a racist. But Mason argues that "one doesn't need to be a racist in order to still be okay with a system that systematically oppresses non-white groups. And that's what's affiliated with the Republican party. It's not that everyone in the party is a racist, it's that the party is not interested in addressing any type of systemic racism."

White voters without a college degree flocked to Trump in the 2016 election and partisan tensions are heightened by the fact that white Americans are expected to become a minority within the next 30 years.

"That's a huge factor," Mason says. "There is a sense of threat that white Americans feel about that. Ultimately, it's going to create a situation in which Republican candidates are going to have a much harder time winning elections and so they really have two options. One is to reach out to racial minorities, or to rig the system."

Around the country, Republican attempts to "rig the system" are also fuelling political division and anger. In North Carolina it started after Republicans won both houses of the state legislature in 2010.

Republican legislators subsequently pushed through a new voter ID law and redrew election districts in their favour. It provoked a fierce backlash. The Moral Mondays movement, led by the Reverend William Barber II, then head of the state chapter of the National Association for the Advancement of Colored People, the NAACP, organised regular rallies to protest against the Republican-led General Assembly at the legislature building in Raleigh.

Barber says he launched the movement because the legislature "attacked everybody, from the teachers to the poor to the sick. Then they attacked voting rights. They knew that voter ID would hurt minorities, women and students. But it wasn't just voter ID. They wanted to roll back same-day registration, early voting. They didn't even want 17 to 18 year olds to preregister to vote. This was an all-out war on the ballot."

The NAACP mounted a legal challenge to the Republican voter ID law and, in 2016 in the federal appeals court, judges struck it down saying the law was designed to "target African-Americans with almost surgical precision." Yet this past December, North Carolina Republicans passed another voter ID law. The NAACP and other voting rights advocates are challenging it again in court.

"Racism is always in play in this country," Barber says. "We tend to talk about racism when something like Charlottesville happens, which is a form of ugly, vile racism. But the racism that is deadly in terms of the long-term health of the country is systemic racism. The kind of racism that people can actually shake your hand and look at you, never call you the n-word, but when they're sitting in their office they pass racist voter suppression."

Voter Fraud and Voter Suppression

Nationwide, 25 states have made it harder to vote since 2010, and 15 passed voter ID laws claiming they were needed to combat voter fraud. Democrats say the claims of fraud are an excuse to suppress the vote and have introduced legislation in Congress to stop it.

Lee Drutman, a senior fellow at the New America think tank, fears that growing doubts about the integrity of the electoral system could lead to violence in the US. "We have this 50/50 politics in which elections can really depend on a few thousand votes here or there," he says. "And both sides have come to believe that the electoral system is not legitimate. On the Republican side it's voter fraud, on the Democratic side it's voter suppression. And when you see political violence across countries it is usually around elections when there's a sense that the elections were not legitimate."

Manipulating the boundaries of an electoral district to ensure it has a majority of voters favouring a party—what is known as gerrymandering—also fuels partisan distrust. Drutman points out: "Gerrymandering, which Republicans have been particularly aggressive at in the last decade, creates this sense that whatever the outcome somebody cheated."

In 2018, Republican candidates for Congress in North Carolina got 50.39 percent of the vote, but won 10 of the state's 13 congressional seats. Last March, the US Supreme Court heard a case challenging Republican gerrymandering in the state. But in June, the court's Republican-appointed majority ruled against the effort to rein in partisan gerrymandering.

According to Andrew Reynolds, a professor at the University of North Carolina, gerrymandering is particularly insidious today because of advances in digital mapping techniques. "They're using computerised maps to literally draw lines around one way streets and tiny little houses in farm country," he says. "You can pick out every house you want to be in a district. And what you are doing is just making sure your party can almost never lose that district."

The real contest in a gerrymandered district is not in the general election, but in the primary contest where candidates vie to be the nominee of the party favoured by the gerrymander. And that fosters partisan extremism, Reynolds says.

"When you create safe seats, the Democrats appeal to the extremes of the Democratic party, the Republicans appeal to the extremes of the Republican part. If districts required you to appeal to the moderate centre then we would see a very different type of Republicans being elected. But when you draw a district that relies upon the primary then they're going to rally the faithful with dog whistles, with racism, with homophobia, with behaviours that create fearfulness about the other, the Mexicans coming in."

Digital Echo-Chambers

Lockwood Phillips, the owner-operator of a conservative radio station that broadcasts to Lenoir County and the surrounding area, is not concerned about gerrymandering in the state. "It's been going on for well over 100 years, and it's business as usual," he says.

But Phillips is bothered by the toxic partisanship in the country. "It's removed a willingness on the part of local voters and participants to sit down and talk, and identify the problems that they have in their immediate community." He also disagrees with the notion that race is at the root of hyper-partisanship and incivility in the US today. "We have racial issues in this country, but they are being solved," he says. "The problem is you've got folks in certain quarters—and I have to say liberal quarters—who don't want that solution because it's a great way to keep the community stirred up."

Instead, Phillips blames polarisation in America on the cellphone and the internet. "The digital environment has oxymoronically, counterintuitively shut down the communications because what happens is people go into their echo chambers," he says.

Phillips's station was the first in North Carolina to carry right-wing radio host Rush Limbaugh and is an affiliate of Fox, President Trump's favourite news outlet. Phillips believes the Mueller report cleared Trump. "It was pretty obvious, there was no effort on the part of Trump to use the Russians or the Russians to use Trump," he says. Mike Parker, of the Sons of Confederate Veterans, feels the same way. According to him, "Mueller's report basically said there was nothing that rose to the level of crime."

"The Mueller report is a Rorschach test for your partisan politics," Drutman argues. "If you're a Democrat you think that there's got to be something criminal in there. If you're Republican you think that Trump is exonerated."

In Drutman's view, these different positions on the Mueller report ultimately reflect a partisan division in America that is rooted in race and identity. "The two parties are fundamentally split over race and identity," he says. "I think if we had partisan polarisation that was purely sectional, North versus South, as we did in the 1850s, we would be on the verge of civil war right now."

3

Partisanship Creates a Healthy Democracy

Salvatore Babones

Salvatore Babones is an American sociologist and an associate professor at the University of Sydney.

In a healthy democracy, voters have clear choices in elections. When politicians are too similar, there is little incentive for citizens to vote. Increasing partisanship in US politics highlights the stark differences between the two major political parties and their candidates. Partisanship and the division it creates between political parties bring choices back to the electorate, which draws voters back to the ballot box. When this happens, American democracy will thrive.

Every four years the country's political elite gets all worked up over politics—and hardly anyone else notices. In the midterm election years, that is. The midterms often feel more like a charity walk-a-thon than a Usain Bolt sprint; sometimes it seems like no one is really "running" at all. The candidates' names may change, but their policies remain the same. Sometimes even the names don't change for decades on end.

This year is different. If you love Brett Kavanaugh, big coal, American manufacturing, tax cuts, and the stock market, vote Republican this November 6. If you hate Brett Kavanaugh, but love the Paris climate accord, peace with Iran, and big government—

"The Great Partisan Divide Is Good for America," by Salvatore Babones, *The National Interest*, October 9, 2018. Reprinted by permission.

and want to see Donald Trump impeached—vote Democrat. Midterm voting hasn't been this easy in decades.

A healthy democracy requires clear choices like these. Political pundits spend hours each day parsing candidates' voting records, but ordinary voters don't. Political pundits love to see the two major parties cooperating to pass major legislation, then going out to the same Washington bars to celebrate together. But for ordinary voters, that makes all politicians look pretty much the same. And if they're all the same, why bother voting at all?

And for several decades, they all did pretty much look the same. There was an elite consensus in Washington that took issue after issue off the table and out of politics. Call it bipartisanship if you want, or call it conspiracy. Either way, for years the American people had little choice over key issues like free trade, bank bailouts, and the federalization of K-12 education. Democrats and Republicans came and went, but the elite agenda just kept moving forward. The return of partisanship threatens all that—and it's about time, too.

As American politics have slowly become more partisan, American voters have started to return to the polls. Voter turnout was consistently high in the 1950s and 1960s as the country grappled with desegregation, civil rights, the Great Society, and the war in Vietnam. Back then, Presidential elections really did have consequences. No 1950s Democrat would have sent the 101st Airborne to integrate Arkansas schools, and no 1960s Republican would have given us Medicare.

Presidential elections mattered much less in the seventies, eighties and nineties. Pierce through the hazy feel-good (or feel-bad) memories of times gone by, and you'll find that Richard Nixon gave us the Environmental Protection Agency, Jimmy Carter ordered the Army into Iran (it's not his fault that their helicopters crashed), and Ronald Reagan of all people presided over one of the biggest expansions in the federal government in history. George H.W. Bush and Bill Clinton together gave us NAFTA and the WTO.

Amidst all this bipartisanship, voting in Presidential elections bottomed out. The only spark in Presidential voter turnout between 1972 and 2004 was the 1992 election contested by the independent Ross Perot. Since the return of partisanship in the 2000s, voter turnout in Presidential elections has climbed back to its postwar average of around 55 percent. That's because as elections have become more partisan, they have become more important. The Trump factor all but assures that voter turnout will soar to a new high in 2020.

Turnout in midterm Congressional elections, by contrast, never bounced back. In fact, it hit a new postwar low in 2014. The reason is simple: gerrymandering. Instead of fighting things out at the polls, the Democrats and (especially) the Republicans prefer to crack and pack the electorate into highly artificial "districts" that provide them with safe, noncompetitive seats. These days, when it comes to congressional elections, the voters don't choose their representatives. The representatives choose their voters.

Bring on the Breitbart

Perhaps the biggest single factor behind the rise of partisanship in the 2000s was the birth of Fox News. Launched just before the 1996 elections, Fox News has been the dominant cable news channel in America since 2002. Its obvious partisan tilt has freed other news outlets, like MSNBC on cable to the *New York Times* in print, to become more openly partisan as well. The idea that the news should be "fair and balanced," so dear to political scientists and media scholars, is now so old hat that it has even been abandoned by Fox News itself.

If you worry that television and newspapers have become too biased, don't even look at the internet. Everyone knows how Breitbart's Steve Bannon went to bat for Donald Trump. But on the other side of the partisan divide, fifty-seven out of fifty-nine major American newspapers endorsed Hillary Clinton, to say nothing of all the progressive websites that relentlessly promoted Bernie Sanders. It's like a return to the 1890s, when the likes of Joseph

Pulitzer and William Randolph Hearst were battling it out for readers with hyper-partisan yellow journalism

Incidentally, voter turnout in the election of 1896 was 79.3 percent, a figure never again reached in US election history. The election pitted the fiery progressive Democrat William Jennings Bryan against the arch-conservative Republican William McKinley. Everyone knew where the candidates stood on the big issues of the day, and they got what they voted for: McKinley, protective tariffs, and the gold standard.

Academics are still debating whether or not those were the right choices. But that they were popular choices was proved in 1900, when McKinley beat Bryan again, this time by an even wider margin. Democracy requires choices, and back then the two major parties offered real choices to the American electorate. Today's return of partisanship means the return of choices. Whoever the Democrats put forward in 2020, one thing is clear: Trump will give the voters a clear choice. And that's just what democracy needs.

4

Heightened Partisanship Increases Civic Engagement and Voter Turnout

Pietro S. Nivola

Pietro S. Nivola is a former senior fellow at the Brookings Institution and served as the vice president and director of governance studies between 2004 and 2008.

Partisanship may be beneficial for American democracy. In partisan politics, the parties' positions on issues and policies are distinct and well defined. The US electorate knows what to expect from its political parties and politicians. Rising partisanship also drives increased civic engagement and interest in elections. As the partisan divide grows, voter participation surges. In this way, American democracy is robust and healthy because of partisanship and is not broken, as some people believe.

From the steps of the Capitol on January 20th, President Barack Obama appealed for an end to the politics of "petty grievances" and "worn-out dogmas." The year 2009 was supposed to mark the dawn of a post-partisan era. With any luck, Democrats and Republicans would stop quarreling, and would finally get down to work together. The time had come, exhorted the new president drawing from Scripture, to lay "childish" polemics aside.

But childish or not, America's partisan politics have remained as stubbornly intense and polarized as ever. To paraphrase more

"In Defense of Partisan Politics," by Pietro S. Nivola, The Brookings Institution, April 8, 2009. Reprinted by permission.

Scripture, the lambs remain unwilling to lie down with the lions. And there are few signs of partisan swords being turned into plowshares. Far from opening a new age of bipartisan comity in the House of Representatives, the president and the Democratic majority received not a single Republican vote in their first big legislative test, the roll call on the so-called American Recovery and Reinvestment Act (the "stimulus"). More recently, not one Republican in the Senate or the House voted for the concurrent resolution on the president's budget. More, not less, of such party-line voting probably lies ahead.

So here's a heretical thought: Maybe, among the many inflated expectations that we attach to the Obama presidency and should temper, those about the advent of "post-partisanship" ought to be lowered, drastically. In other words, get over it. The rough-and-tumble of our party politics is here to stay. What's more—and this is even greater heresy—not everything about that fact of political life is horrible.

Majoritarianism

The Democratic and Republican parties today are each more cemented in their ideologies and more distinct than they were a generation ago. In Congress, party lines used to be blurred by the existence of so-called liberal Republicans and truly conservative Democrats. Now those factions are dwindling species. Why they are dying out is a long story that has been the object of an extensive study titled *Red and Blue Nation?* cosponsored by Brookings and the Hoover Institution at Stanford University. For present purposes, suffice it to recognize that the disputes between Republicans and Democrats are about more than "petty grievances" (though there are plenty of them, too); the party differences run deep and fundamentally reflect differing convictions held by large blocs of voters, not just their elected representatives. An example: Whereas a staggering 84 percent of Democrats seem to believe "it's the government's responsibility to make sure that everyone in the United States has adequate health care," only 34 percent of

Republicans evidently concur, according to a reputable national poll taken last November.

Because both parties are more cohesive, they are also more disciplined. If you are a member of Congress and you basically agree with your party's position on most salient issues, why defect to the other side on key votes? Americans of the baby-boom generation are not accustomed to seeing this high degree of party unity. They remember the old days when the main way to do business on Capitol Hill was to cobble together ad-hoc coalitions. Want a civil rights bill? Get northern Democrats and Republican moderates on your side, and hope that you have enough votes to overpower the conservative phalanx of southern Democrats and states'-rights Republicans. Want more money for the Vietnam War in the 1960s? Combine solid support from that bipartisan conservative bloc with plenty of other hawkish stalwarts in both parties (think reliable GOP loyalists like Everett Dirksen but also Scoop Jackson Democrats), and you'd get the funds.

Increasingly, the contemporary party system bears scant resemblance to the one that prevailed a half-century ago. What it resembles instead is politics in most other periods of American history, for example the late nineteenth century when the two parties were also internally coherent and keenly at odds. During such periods, the American parties have behaved more like political parties in parliamentary regimes—where the in-party (the governing majority) rules, and the out-party (the minority) consistently forms a loyal opposition.

Notice this distinctive feature of the parliamentary model: Not only can the majority, voting in lockstep, prevail with no help from opposition members; all it needs on board in order to legislate is a simple majority of the legislators. Supermajorities—the requirement in the US Senate to override a filibuster—are never the norm. A parliamentary system, in other words, operates much like our congressional budget reconciliation process where as little as a one-vote margin in the House and as little as 51 votes in the Senate suffice to adopt a bill.

There is much handwringing about the trend toward majoritarian—that is, parliamentary-style—politics in the United States. Democrats moaned when the GOP, led by George W. Bush, drove tax cuts through Congress on nearly a party-line vote with Vice President Cheney casting the tie-breaker. Now, Republicans will groan if the Obama administration and the Democratic congressional leadership opt to use the reconciliation procedure to ram health-care reform into law.

But is all the lamentation justified?

Accountability

One of the advantages of parliamentary democracy is that the electorate knows what to expect. What you see (or vote for) is what you get. As America becomes parliamentary, if voters elect a Republican president and congressional majority, here's a good bet: Tax cuts will be on the way. If voters elect a Democratic president and congressional majority—running on a party platform that declares universal health care to be a "moral imperative"—guess what? Health-care legislation to extend coverage will happen. Now, granted one can debate the policy merits of either party's priorities. Robotic tax-cutting runs up deficits—and so almost certainly will health care that covers everybody. But if the voters have explicitly empowered their elected officials to do either of these things, who are "we" to stand in the way?

Further, the voters have plenty of opportunity to change their minds. If they decide that mistakes are being made—or that they prefer an alternative agenda to the one being proffered by the party in power—they can throw the rascals out. Indeed, in this country, unlike practically every other democracy, the public gets a chance to entertain that option with extraordinary frequency: every two years.

Nor, from the standpoint of democratic theory, is it easy to make an airtight case for why Congress and the president should be forced to muster supermajorities to enact their most important priorities. Ours, like any sound democracy, has to balance principles of majority rule with minority rights. But a political order in which technically just over 7 percent of a legislature—that is, a sub-group that possibly represents as little as 10 percent of the population—can have the last word, as our Senate arithmetic can imply, raises serious questions of democratic accountability and even legitimacy. Let's face it: making a regular practice of putting, in effect, veto-power in the hands of a minority is hard to square with a government of the people, by the people, for the people.

The Virtues of a Choice, Not an Echo

There is one other thing to say in defense of heightened partisanship: It has succeeded in making elections more interesting.

Voters have a tendency to become indifferent and apathetic when asked to choose between alternatives that display not "a dime's worth of difference," as the old saying went about our two-party system during the heyday of bipartisan comingling.

By contrast, as Marc J. Hetherington of Vanderbilt University demonstrates in a key chapter of *Red and Blue Nation?*, voter participation has surged as the partisan divide has grown sharper.

The electorate is not turned off by the chasm, and contestation, between the parties. On the contrary, Hetherington finds, the polarized political parties have animated voters of all stripes—liberals, conservatives, and moderates. Growing civic engagement and voter turnouts are hallmarks of a vibrant democracy, not of a "broken" one.

5

Extreme Political Polarization Harms US Democracy

Jennifer Lynn McCoy

Jennifer Lynn McCoy is a professor of political science and the founding director of the Global Studies Institute at Georgia State University.

Extreme polarization divides society into distinct political sides. As each side increasingly views the other as a threat to the country and their way of life, they become more willing to accept authoritarian behavior to keep their party in power. They also become more willing to support undemocratic methods to remove the opposing party from power. In this way, extreme polarization damages democracy. Research shows that citizens can protect democracy by understanding the factors that contribute to extreme polarization and spotting the early warning signs of democratic damage. To reduce negative polarization, both political leaders and citizens need to play a role. Embracing generosity and openness over blame and vilification, the United States can mend the bitter polarization that threatens democracy.

"Extreme Political Polarization Weakens Democracy—Can the US Avoid That Fate?" by Jennifer Lynn McCoy, The Conversation Media Group Ltd, October 31, 2018. https://theconversation.com/extreme-political-polarization-weakens-democracy-can-the-us-avoid-that-fate-105540.

The midterm elections are approaching during one of the most polarized moments in recent American politics.

A collaborative research project I led on polarized democracies around the world examines the processes by which societies divide into political "tribes" and democracy is harmed.

Based on a study of 11 countries including the US, Turkey, Hungary, Venezuela, Thailand and others, we found that when political leaders cast their opponents as immoral or corrupt, they create "us" and "them" camps—called by political scientists and psychologists "in-groups" and "out-groups"—in the society.

In this tribal dynamic, each side views the other "out group" party with increasing distrust, bias and enmity.

Perceptions that "If you win, I lose" grow. Each side views the other political party and their supporters as a threat to the nation or their way of life if that other political party is in power.

For that reason, the incumbent's followers tolerate more illiberal and increasingly authoritarian behavior to stay in power, while the opponents are more and more willing to resort to undemocratic means to remove them from power.

This damages democracy.

Are Americans now stuck in animosity and anger that will undermine democracy, or can the nation pull out of it?

Politicians Divide

Our research finds that severe polarization is affected by three primary factors.

First, it is often stimulated by the rhetoric of political leaders who exploit the real grievances of voters. These politicians choose divisive issues to highlight in order to pursue their own political agenda.

In other words, what a leader says is as important as what she or he does.

Since launching his campaign, President Donald Trump has vilified so-called external enemies such as "criminal and rapist" Mexican immigrants, terrorist Muslims and foreign allies out to drain America's coffers through "unfair trade deficits." Now, the president is targeting internal enemies.

He has famously labeled the media "the enemy of the people" and recently accused the Democrats of unleashing an "angry mob" unfit to govern.

Such unprecedented attacks by a president of the United States seemed designed to discredit his critics and delegitimize his political opponents. But they also trigger the dynamics of polarized politics by reinforcing the notion that politics is an "us versus them" contest.

By August 2017, just eight months after Trump took office, three-quarters of Republicans had negative views of Democrats, and 70 percent of Democrats viewed Republicans negatively.

This was a large increase compared with the mid-1990s, when about 20 percent of each party had unfavorable views of the other party.

Even more disturbing for democracy, roughly half of voters of each party say the other party makes them feel afraid, and growing numbers view the policies of the other party as a threat to the nation.

America's recent political polarization did not begin with Trump. It has been growing since the 1990s and accelerated under President Barack Obama, when the Tea Party formed in reaction to his election, and bipartisanship broke down in the Congress.

By 2016, 45 percent of Republicans felt threatened by Democratic policies, and 41 percent of Democrats viewed Republican policies as a threat, up nearly 10 points in just two years.

Our research shows that in extreme polarization, people feel distant from and suspicious of the "other" camp. At the same time, they feel loyal to, and trusting of, their own camp—without examining their biases or factual basis of their information.

Although this is a common phenomenon long identified by social psychology, it is even more pronounced in the age of social media 24-hour news cycles and more politicized media outlets who repeat and amplify the political attacks.

Most dangerously, words can unleash actual violence by avid supporters seeking approval from the leader or simply inspired to carry out an attack against the designated "enemy," as we saw when supporters of Hugo Chávez in Venezuela attacked a media mogul whom Chávez had labeled public enemy number one.

Similarly, last week an avid Trump supporter sent pipe bomb mailers to prominent Trump opponents, and the killings in a synagogue in Pittsburgh were carried out by a man who used similar language to Trump's assertion that the US was being invaded by a caravan of Central Americans.

Polarization, though, is a two-way street.

Both Sides Now

How the political opposition reacts is the second factor explaining the impact of polarization on democracy.

If the opposition returns the bitter rhetoric with similar political hardball and demonizing language, they risk locking in place a cycle that leads to entrenching the politics of polarization.

A perceived political win may in fact prove to be an eventual defeat. That happened in 2013 when the Democratic Party changed the long-standing rule that nominees to federal judgeships needed 60 Senate votes to end debate and move to a confirmation vote.

To overcome Republican obstruction under Obama, the Democrats who held a majority in the Senate at the time abandoned that rule and decreed that only 51 votes would be needed for all federal judgeships—except the Supreme Court.

Eventually the majority party becomes once again the minority. That's what happened when Republicans gained the majority in 2014 and blocked Obama's last nomination for a Supreme Court justice.

When Democrats retaliated by filibustering Trump's first nominee for the Supreme Court, the Republican Party escalated the fight and abolished the century-old filibuster rule even for the highest court in the land. They approved Justice Brett Kavanaugh with only a single Democratic vote.

Backing Away from Polarization

The third, and most difficult, obstacle is what our research found about the underlying basis of polarization.

When countries polarize around rifts that reflect unresolved debates present at the country's formation, then that polarization is most likely to be enduring and harmful.

The US was founded on unequal citizenship rights for African-Americans, Native Americans and women. As these groups reasserted their rights in the 1960s civil rights movement and the 1970s women's movement, polarization around these rights and changing group status grew.

The same is true for the growing diversity of religion, gender and ethnicity in the workplace and society since the 1980s, which has become an added polarizing issue in US politics.

Can the US overcome the dynamics of polarization, where certain phenomena—divisive and demonizing rhetoric, tit-for-tat political retribution and long-standing unresolved rifts—lead to diminished democracy?

Our research shows that the most democratic of actions—participating in elections—is exactly the thing to do to help reduce polarization.

To avoid deepening the state of division and distrust that seems to pervade our society, both political leaders and citizens must play a part. Simply withdrawing from politics is not effective.

Citizens can protect themselves and their democracy by being aware of the political and psychological workings of polarization and the early warning signs of democratic erosion.

They can refuse to participate in the trap of demonizing politics, while insisting on voting massively against those who use polarizing methods.

Political leaders should be conscious that their words and actions can advance, prevent or reverse severe polarization.

For those who prioritize winning for their team above all, the realization that they will eventually be the losers of their re-engineered rules should be sobering—whether it is eliminating the filibuster in the US Senate or the right to gerrymander electoral districts.

For those who have a broader perspective focused on the collective interests and welfare of the society, understanding the logic of polarization that blocks cooperative problem-solving could instill the courage to cross the divide rather than reciprocate pernicious polarizing strategies.

The ultimate solution to depolarize the contentiousness around national identity and citizenship rights that divides the US, however, requires addressing these debates head-on.

With a spirit of inquiry, generosity and openness, rather than blame and vilification, the US can move past the bitter divisions that threaten the democratic foundations of the country.

6

A Divided Government Does Not Always Lead to Legislative Gridlock

Jeffrey D. Grynaviski

Jeffrey D. Grynaviski is a professor of political science at Wayne State University.

History shows that divided government does not always lead to legislative gridlock. In previous Congresses in which opposing political parties controlled the House and Senate, the results have varied. In the 98th Congress (1983–1985), legislators compromised on bipartisan legislation, including amendments to preserve Social Security that increased taxes and cut benefits. In contrast, in the 112th Congress (2011–2013), compromise was rare, and a divided government almost crippled Congress. The growing political polarization in recent years has made compromise more difficult to reach. Will President Trump pursue bipartisan compromise, and will congressional Democrats be willing to make concessions? The answer is unclear.

Congress seemingly hasn't accomplished much apart from a tax cut and criminal justice reform since the election of President Trump in 2016, despite all three branches being controlled by the GOP.

"Congress Used to Pass Bipartisan Legislation—Will It Ever Again?" by Jeffrey D. Grynaviski, The Conversation Media Group Ltd, January 4, 2019. https://theconversation.com/congress-used-to-pass-bipartisan-legislation-will-it-ever-again-107134.

Will that record get even worse now that the US has divided government?

As a political scientist who studies Congress, I find it tempting to look to political history for guidance on what could happen with the new Congress.

Yet, if you look at the previous two instances since World War II where the United States had this form of divided government, the implications for legislative productivity could not be more different.

Some Are Productive

The two other Congresses whose political makeup was closest to today's 116th were the 98th, which sat from 1983–1985, and the 112th Congress, which sat from 2011–2013.

The common denominators for these three Congresses are that the incumbent president is up for re-election, the Senate is controlled by the president's party and the House of Representatives is controlled by the opposition.

During the 98th Congress, Republican Ronald Reagan was president, with his party holding a 55-to-45 majority in the Senate and a whopping 103-seat deficit in the House, where Massachusetts Democrat Tip O'Neill was speaker.

Historians generally hold the 98th Congress in high regard for its bipartisanship during a period of divided government. As reported by the political scientist David Mayhew in his landmark study, *Divided We Govern*, its most important legislative accomplishments included:

- The declaration of Martin Luther King's birthday as a federal holiday;
- Amendments to Social Security to preserve the pension system's solvency that increased taxes and cut benefits;
- A major revision of the federal criminal code that included increased penalties for drug trafficking and terrorism;
- Reduction of the deficit through a package of spending cuts and tax hikes.

Looking beyond these highlights, the total of 667 laws enacted by the 98th Congress was well above the historical average of about 552 passed per Congress since the early 1970s.

Others Are Unproductive

Democrat Barack Obama was president during the more recent 112th Congress.

Following the Republican midterm sweep in 2010, Democrats held a 53 (including independents who caucused with Democrats) to 47 majority in the Senate, but trailed Republicans by 49 seats in the House.

This Congress arguably exhibited the most intransigent partisan divisions of the post-war period.

According to the Brookings Institute's Vital Statistics on Congress, the 283 laws passed by the 112th were the fewest enacted by any Congress going back at least until the Korean War.

One thing should be pointed out in defense of Congress' low productivity in recent years. Congressional scholar David Mayhew has written in Politico that counting the number of enacted laws is an overly simplistic measure of productivity.

That's because Congress has increasingly turned to so-called "omnibus" legislation, or legislative packages that sweep up lots of smaller measures into one large bill.

As a result, one important bill passed by Congress today might reasonably be considered as equal to multiple major successes for a previous Congress. For example, Mayhew argues that the Budget Control Act of 2011 and the American Taxpayers Relief Act of 2012, both of which attempted to address the budgetary crises during Obama's first term, were important omnibus legislative accomplishments.

Nevertheless, the contrast between the two Congresses is stark.

Democrats and Republicans in the 98th Congress compromised to keep the country's entitlement system solvent for decades.

The 112th Congress, on the other hand, was dominated by partisan brinkmanship over debts and deficits that led to the downgrading of the United States' credit rating, a key measure of the economy's health.

Growing Divisions Are Key

Arguably, the most important difference between the 98th and 112th Congress was the sharp increase in ideological polarization between Democrat and Republican politicians that made compromise increasingly difficult.

During the early 1980s, many southern white voters retained their loyalty to conservative Democrats in the House and Senate who had heretofore resisted the civil rights movement and integration.

As a result, there was a constituency within the Democratic Party in Congress that was more ideologically predisposed to cut a deal with Reagan. It is notable, for example, that during the 98th Congress, Social Security reform included both tax increases—which Democrats liked—and cuts to benefits—which Republicans liked.

However, it was also in the early 1980s that conservative politicians and voters in the South increasingly aligned with the Republican Party. Largely because of this partisan realignment, by the mid-1990s there was little—if any—overlap in the ideological convictions of Democrats and Republicans in Congress.

In other words, from the 98th to the 112th Congress, fewer and fewer members of the two major parties agreed on potential resolutions to the issues of the day. Compromise became harder to reach.

Given the current political climate, it is difficult to imagine a reprise of the productive 98th Congress. Would President Trump agree to increased payroll taxes to pay for Social Security and Medicare? Would Speaker Pelosi agree to benefit cuts to those programs? Unlikely.

They Did a Lot

It is not at all clear how the controversies surrounding President Trump will affect the behavior of the new Congress.

Probably the closest historical analogues are the various Congresses that exercised strong oversight of the president.

The 93rd Congress (1973–1974) held hearings on Nixon's role in Watergate; the 100th Congress (1987–1988) conducted an investigation into the Iran-Contra scandal during the second Reagan administration; and the 106th Congress (1999–2000) exercised their oversight when the House voted to impeach President Bill Clinton and the Senate failed to impeach him over the Monica Lewinsky scandal.

All three Congresses maintained reasonably high levels of legislative productivity based on the total number of enactments and the number of important bills that were passed. That happened despite the government in all three cases being divided.

The 93rd Congress' accomplishments included passage of the War Powers Act; creation of the modern congressional budget system; and passage of the United States' first meaningful system of campaign finance regulation.

The 100th Congress passed significant enhancements to the landmark Clean Water Act of 1972; legislation to maintain and upgrade the nation's transportation systems; and ratification of an arms treaty, which required the US and Soviet Russia to destroy a substantial percentage of their nuclear weapons.

The 106th Congress passed landmark banking reform legislation, normalized trade relations with China and wrote rules governing litigation over anticipated problems arising from the turn of the millennium, or Y2K.

How Much Will They Do?

Does the return of divided government in the current Congress mean not much will happen over the next two years? On this question, history doesn't provide clear guidance.

In terms of legislative productivity, the divided 98th Congress is a positive example of Democrats and Republicans cooperating to do the people's business. But during the 112th, divided government almost crippled Congress.

Because of today's high levels of partisan polarization, the unproductive 112th Congress probably provides the best framework for thinking about what to expect in the next two years.

Yet it is also the case that bipartisan compromise was part of Reagan's pathway to re-election in 1984. It's an open question whether that is a route that President Trump wants to pursue—and whether congressional Democrats are more willing to make concessions in order to chalk up legislative victories of their own than the Republicans were during the 112th.

7

Identity Politics Creates Deep Divisions

Amy Chua

Amy Chua is the John M. Duff Professor of Law at Yale University and author of several books, including Political Tribes: Group Instinct and the Fate of Nations.

Fifty years ago, the civil rights movement called for national unity, equal opportunity, and inclusion for all. Idealists promoted an America that looked past ethnicity, race, religion, and gender to see all humans equally. However, as some conservative groups used "colorblindness" to oppose policies intended to minimize racial inequalities, a new movement of identity politics began to emerge that focused on differences, exclusion, and division. Stuck in the division of identity politics, no one is standing up for an American identity that unites all of the country's many subgroups together.

We are at an unprecedented moment in America.

For the first time in US history, white Americans are faced with the prospect of becoming a minority in their "own country." While many in our multicultural cities may well celebrate the "browning of America" as a welcome step away from "white supremacy," it's safe to say that large numbers of American whites are more anxious about this phenomenon, whether they admit it or not. Tellingly, a 2012 study showed that more than half of

"How America's Identity Politics Went from Inclusion to Division," by Amy Chua, Professor of Law, Yale University. Reprinted by permission.

white Americans believe that "whites have replaced blacks as the 'primary victims of discrimination.'"

Meanwhile, the coming demographic shift has done little to allay minority concerns about discrimination. A recent survey found that 43% of black Americans do not believe America will ever make the changes necessary to give blacks equal rights. Most disconcertingly, hate crimes have increased 20% in the wake of the 2016 election.

When groups feel threatened, they retreat into tribalism. When groups feel mistreated and disrespected, they close ranks and become more insular, more defensive, more punitive, more us-versus-them.

In America today, every group feels this way to some extent. Whites and blacks, Latinos and Asians, men and women, Christians, Jews, and Muslims, straight people and gay people, liberals and conservatives—all feel their groups are being attacked, bullied, persecuted, discriminated against.

Of course, one group's claims to feeling threatened and voiceless are often met by another group's derision because it discounts their own feelings of persecution—but such is political tribalism.

This—combined with record levels of inequality—is why we now see identity politics on both sides of the political spectrum. And it leaves the United States in a perilous new situation: almost no one is standing up for an America without identity politics, for an American identity that transcends and unites all the country's many subgroups.

This is certainly true of the American left today.

Fifty years ago, the rhetoric of pro–civil rights, Great Society liberals was, in its dominant voices, expressly group transcending, framed in the language of national unity and equal opportunity.

In his most famous speech, Dr. Martin Luther King Jr. proclaimed: "When the architects of our republic wrote the magnificent words of the Constitution and the Declaration of Independence, they were signing a promissory note to which every American was to fall heir. This note was a promise that all men—yes, black men as well as white men—would be guaranteed the unalienable rights of life, liberty, and the pursuit of happiness."

King's ideals—the ideals of the American Left that captured the imagination and hearts of the public and led to real change—transcended group divides and called for an America in which skin color didn't matter.

Leading liberal philosophical movements of that era were similarly group blind and universalist in character. John Rawls's enormously influential *A Theory of Justice*, published in 1971, called on people to imagine themselves in an "original position," behind a "veil of ignorance," in which they could decide on their society's basic principles without regard to "race, gender, religious affiliation, [or] wealth."

At roughly the same time, the idea of universal human rights proliferated, advancing the dignity of every individual as the foundation of a just international order.

Thus, although the Left was always concerned with the oppression of minorities and the rights of disadvantaged groups, the dominant ideals in this period tended to be group blind, often cosmopolitan, with many calling for transcending not just ethnic, racial, and gender barriers but national boundaries as well.

Perhaps in reaction to Reaganism, and a growing awareness that "colorblindness" was being used by conservatives to oppose policies intended to redress racial inequities, a new movement began to unfold on the left in the 1980s and 1990s—a movement emphasizing group consciousness, group identity, and group claims.

Many on the left had become acutely aware that color blindness was being used by conservatives to oppose policies intended to redress historical wrongs and persisting racial inequities.

Many also began to notice that the leading liberal figures in America, whether in law, government, or academia, were predominantly white men and that the neutral "group-blind" invisible hand of the market wasn't doing much to correct long-standing imbalances.

With the collapse of the Soviet Union, the anti-capitalist economic preoccupations of the old Left began to take a backseat to a new way of understanding oppression: the politics of redistribution was replaced by a "politics of recognition." Modern identity politics was born.

As Oberlin professor Sonia Kruks writes, "What makes identity politics a significant departure from earlier [movements] is its demand for recognition on the basis of the very grounds on which recognition has previously been denied: it is qua women, qua blacks, qua lesbians that groups demand recognition ... The demand is not for inclusion within the fold of 'universal humankind' ... nor is it for respect 'in spite of' one's differences. Rather, what is demanded is respect for oneself as different."

But identity politics, with its group-based rhetoric, did not initially become the mainstream position of the Democratic Party.

At the 2004 Democratic National Convention in Boston, Barack Obama famously declared, "There's not a black America and white America and Latino America and Asian America; there's the United States of America."

A decade and a half later, we are very far from Obama's America.

For today's Left, blindness to group identity is the ultimate sin, because it masks the reality of group hierarchies and oppression in America.

It's just a fact that whites, and specifically white male Protestants, dominated America for most of its history, often violently, and that this legacy persists. The stubborn persistence of racial inequality in the wake of Barack Obama's supposedly "post-racial" presidency has left many young progressives disillusioned with the narratives of racial progress that were popular among liberals just a few years ago.

When a grand jury failed to indict a white cop who was videotaped choking a black man to death, black writer Brit Bennett captured this growing mistrust in an essay entitled, "I Don't Know What to Do with Good White People":

> *We all want to believe in progress, in history that marches forward in a neat line, in transcended differences and growing acceptance, in how good the good white people have become ... I don't think Darren Wilson or Daniel Pantaleo set out to kill black men. I'm sure the cops who arrested my father meant well. But what good are your good intentions if they kill us?*

For the Left, identity politics has long been a means to "confront rather than obscure the uglier aspects of American history and society."

But in recent years, whether because of growing strength or growing frustration with the lack of progress, the Left has upped the ante. A shift in tone, rhetoric, and logic has moved identity politics away from inclusion—which had always been the Left's watchword—toward exclusion and division. As a result, many on the left have turned against universalist rhetoric (for example, All Lives Matter), viewing it as an attempt to erase the specificity of the experience and oppression of historically marginalized minorities.

The new exclusivity is partly epistemological, claiming that out-group members cannot share in the knowledge possessed by in-group members ("You can't understand X because you are white"; "You can't understand Y because you're not a woman"; "You can't speak about Z because you're not queer"). The idea of "cultural appropriation" insists, among other things, "These are our group's symbols, traditions, patrimony, and out-group members have no right to them."

For much of the Left today, anyone who speaks in favor of group blindness is on the other side, indifferent to or even guilty of oppression. For some, especially on college campuses, anyone who doesn't swallow the anti-oppression orthodoxy hook, line, and sinker—anyone who doesn't acknowledge "white supremacy" in America—is a racist.

When liberal icon Bernie Sanders told supporters, "It's not good enough for somebody to say, 'Hey, I'm a Latina, vote for me,'" Quentin James, a leader of Hillary Clinton's outreach efforts to people of color, retorted that Sanders's "comments regarding identity politics suggest he may be a white supremacist, too."

Once identity politics gains momentum, it inevitably subdivides, giving rise to ever-proliferating group identities demanding recognition.

Today, there is an ever-expanding vocabulary of identity on the left. Facebook now lists more than fifty gender designations from which users can choose, from genderqueer to intersex to pangender.

Or take the acronym LGBTQ. Originally LGB, variants over the years have ranged from GLBT to LGBTI to LGBTQQIAAP as preferred terminology shifted and identity groups quarreled about who should be included and who come first.

Because the Left is always trying to outleft the last Left, the result can be a zero-sum competition over which group is the least privileged, an "Oppression Olympics" often fragmenting progressives and setting them against each other.

Although inclusivity is presumably still the ultimate goal, the contemporary Left is pointedly exclusionary.

During a Black Lives Matter protest at the DNC held in Philadelphia in July 2016, a protest leader announced that "this is a black and brown resistance march," asking white allies to "appropriately take [their] place in the back of this march."

The war on "cultural appropriation" is rooted in the belief that groups have exclusive rights to their own histories, symbols, and traditions. Thus, many on the left today would consider it an offensive act of privilege for, say, a straight white man to write a novel featuring a gay Latina as the main character.

Transgressions are called out daily on social media; no one is immune. Beyoncé was criticized for wearing what looked like a traditional Indian bridal outfit; Amy Schumer, in turn, was criticized for making a parody of Beyoncé's *Formation*, a song about the black female experience. Students at Oberlin complained of a vendor's "history of blurring the line between culinary diversity and cultural appropriation by modifying the recipes without respect for certain Asian countries' cuisines." And a student op-ed at Louisiana State University claimed that white women styling their eyebrows to look thicker—like "a lot of ethnic women"—was "a prime example of the cultural appropriation in this country."

Not everyone on the Left is happy with the direction that identity politics has taken. Many are dismayed by the focus on cultural appropriation. As a progressive Mexican American law student put it, "If we allowed ourselves to be hurt by a costume, how could we manage the trauma of an eviction notice?"

He added: "Liberals have cried wolf too many times. If everything is racist and sexist, nothing is. When Trump, the real wolf, came along, no one listened."

As a candidate, Donald Trump famously called for "a total and complete shutdown of Muslims entering the United States," described illegal Mexican immigrants as "rapists," and referred disparagingly to an Indiana-born federal judge as "Mexican," accusing the judge of having "an inherent conflict of interest" rendering him unfit to preside over a suit against Trump.

Making the argument that Trump used identity politics to win the White House is like shooting fish in a barrel. But us-versus-them, anti-Muslim, anti-immigrant sentiments were bread and butter for most conservatives on the 2016 campaign trail. Senator Marco Rubio compared the war with Islam to America's "war with Nazis," and even moderate Republicans like Jeb Bush advocated for a religious test to allow Christian refugees to enter the country preferentially.

We are also seeing on the right—particularly the alt-right—political tribalism directed against minorities perceived as "too successful." For example, Steve Bannon, Trump's former White House chief strategist, has complained that America's "engineering schools are all full of people from South Asia and East Asia ... They've come in here to take these jobs" while Americans "can't get engineering degrees ... [and] can't get a job."

This brings us to the most striking feature of today's right-wing political tribalism: the white identity politics that has mobilized around the idea of whites as an endangered, discriminated-against group.

In part this development carries forward a long tradition of white tribalism in America. But white identity politics has also gotten a tremendous recent boost from the Left, whose relentless berating, shaming, and bullying might have done more damage than good.

One Trump voter claimed that "maybe I'm just so sick of being called a bigot that my anger at the authoritarian left has pushed me to support this seriously flawed man." "The Democratic party," said Bill Maher, "made the white working man feel like your problems aren't real because you're 'mansplaining' and check your privilege. You know, if your life sucks, your problems are real." When blacks blame today's whites for slavery or ask for reparations, many white Americans feel as though they are being attacked for the sins of other generations.

Or consider this blog post in the *American Conservative*, worth quoting at length because of the light it sheds:

> *I'm a white guy. I'm a well-educated intellectual who enjoys small arthouse movies, coffeehouses and classic blues. If you didn't know any better, you'd probably mistake me for a lefty urban hipster.*
>
> *And yet. I find some of the alt-right stuff exerts a pull even on me. Even though I'm smart and informed enough to see through it. It's seductive because I am not a person with any power or privilege, and yet I am constantly bombarded with messages telling me that I'm a cancer, I'm a problem, everything is my fault.*
>
> *I am very lower middle class. I've never owned a new car, and do my own home repairs as much as I can to save money. I cut my own grass, wash my own dishes, buy my clothes from Walmart. I have no clue how I will ever be able to retire. But oh, brother, to hear the media tell it, I am just drowning in unearned power and privilege, and America will be a much brighter, more loving, more peaceful nation when I finally just keel over and die.*
>
> *Trust me: After all that, some of the alt-right stuff feels like a warm, soothing bath. A "safe space," if you will. I recoil from the uglier stuff, but some of it— the "hey, white guys are actually*

okay, you know! Be proud of yourself, white man!" stuff is really VERY seductive, and it is only with some intellectual effort that I can resist the pull ... If it's a struggle for someone like me to resist the pull, I imagine it's probably impossible for someone with less education or cultural exposure.

Just as the Left's exclusionary identity politics is ironic in light of the Left's ostensible demands for inclusivity, so too is the emergence of a "white" identity politics on the right.

For decades, the Right has claimed to be a bastion of individualism, a place where those who rejected the divisive identity politics of the Left found a home.

For this reason, conservatives typically paint the emergence of white identity as having been forced on them by the tactics of the Left. As one political commentator puts it, "feeling as though they are under perpetual attack for the color of their skin, many on the right have become defiant of their whiteness, allowing it into their individual politics in ways they have not for generations."

At its core, the problem is simple but fundamental. While black Americans, Asian Americans, Hispanic Americans, Jewish Americans, and many others are allowed—indeed, encouraged—to feel solidarity and take pride in their racial or ethnic identity, white Americans have for the last several decades been told they must never, ever do so.

People want to see their own tribe as exceptional, as something to be deeply proud of; that's what the tribal instinct is all about. For decades now, nonwhites in the United States have been encouraged to indulge their tribal instincts in just this way, but, at least publicly, American whites have not.

On the contrary, if anything, they have been told that their white identity is something no one should take pride in. "I get it," says Christian Lander, creator of the popular satirical blog Stuff White People Like, "as a straight white male, I'm the worst thing on Earth."

But the tribal instinct is not so easy to suppress. As Vassar professor Hua Hsu put it in an *Atlantic* essay called "The End of

White America?" the "result is a racial pride that dares not speak its name, and that defines itself through cultural cues instead."

In combination with the profound demographic transformation now taking place in America, this suppressed urge on the part of many white Americans—to feel solidarity and pride in their group identity, as others are allowed to do—has created an especially fraught set of tribal dynamics in the United States today.

Just after the 2016 election, a former Never Trumper explained his change of heart in the *Atlantic*: "My college-age daughter constantly hears talk of white privilege and racial identity, of separate dorms for separate races (somewhere in heaven Martin Luther King Jr is hanging his head and crying) … I hate identity politics, [but] when everything is about identity politics, is the left really surprised that on Tuesday millions of white Americans … voted as 'white'? If you want identity politics, identity politics is what you will get."

8

Ties to Political Party Are Stronger Than Race, Gender, or Ethnic Heritage

Milenko Martinovich

Milenko Martinovich is the deputy director of social science communications at Stanford University.

According to recent research, Americans' connection to their political party is stronger than connections to race, religion, or ethnic heritage. This strong connection is responsible for the increasing level of political polarization across the country. The strong ties to political parties exist because support for a political party is a deliberate, individual choice, not a factor decided at birth like race and ethnicity. Therefore, alignment with a political party can be seen as a more accurate representation of a person's true self and belief. The partisan bond is not uniquely American but exists in other democracies worldwide.

The self-defining characteristics that Americans hold dear include their racial and cultural heritage, the language they speak and their choice of worship.

But the strongest attachment, according to recent research from a Stanford scholar, is Americans' connection to their political party. And the strength of that partisan bond—stronger than race, religion or ethnicity—has amplified the level of political polarization in the US, the researchers said.

"Americans' Partisan Identities Are Stronger Than Race and Ethnicity, Stanford Scholar Finds," by Milenko Martinovich, Stanford University, August 31, 2017. Reprinted by permission.

The study, co-authored by Shanto Iyengar, a professor of communication and political science at Stanford, and appearing in the *European Journal of Political Research*, finds this increasing partisan divide present not only in America, but in other well-established democracies as well.

The Reasons Why

So why does "partyism," as the researchers refer to it, trump other social identifiers like gender, race, religion, language and ethnicity—affiliations many Americans value highly?

One reason, the researchers find, is that who you support politically is your choice while factors like your race and ethnicity are assigned at birth. Therefore, because support for a political party is a deliberate decision for an individual, it's viewed as a choice that more accurately reflects who that person truly is. "Because partisan affiliation is voluntary, it is a much more informative measure of attitudes and belief structures than, for example, knowing what skin color someone has," the study states.

Another reason is that—unlike race, religion and gender, where social norms dictate behavior—there are few, if any, constraints on the expression of hostility toward people who adhere to opposing political ideologies, the researchers said. For example, certain words are out-of-bounds when directed toward people of specific races or genders. But these boundaries don't really apply in a partisan environment and, in fact, boorish behavior can actually be encouraged by party leaders.

"There are no corresponding pressures to moderate disapproval of political opponents," the study states. "In fact, the rhetoric and behavior of party leaders suggests to voters that it is perfectly acceptable to treat opponents with disdain. In this sense, individuals have greater freedom to discriminate against out-party supporters."

The researchers also cite the frequency of election campaigns and negative attack advertisements as other causes for growth of this partisan divide.

The Trust Game

To measure levels of partisanship, the researchers used a behavioral game involving donating money to individuals based on profiles that included, among other information, their political affiliation. The study involved more than 4,000 participants from Belgium, Spain, the United Kingdom and the United States.

The game's results revealed that players from all four countries exhibited strong bonds with politically like-minded players while expressing "significant dislike for members of the political opposition," the paper states. What the researchers also found significant was that this partisan behavior appeared both in divided societies, like Belgium and Spain, where rifts along social lines run deep, and in integrated societies, like the UK and US, where those social divides are less prevalent.

Among US participants, the researchers found Americans' animosity toward players from opposing political viewpoints was stronger than favoritism shown toward politically like-minded players. In other words, they disliked their enemies even more than they liked their friends. American players provided an 8 percent bonus to players with the same partisan affiliation. However, Republican participants were penalized 10 percent by Democrats and Democratic participants were penalized 16 percent by Republicans. According to Iyengar, "This finding suggests that partisans are motivated more by out-group animosity than in-group favoritism."

Showing Their Support

The widespread behavior suggests that Americans are not alone in having their partisan beliefs occupy a major identity role.

But where they did find Americans to be distinct was in their outward display of partisan identities. Americans affix bumper stickers to their cars and place yard signs outside their homes advertising their political preferences, a behavior uncommon in other societies where citizens tend to keep those views to themselves. "American campaigns feature greater involvement on the part of ordinary citizens," Iyengar said. "Campaigns also last much longer than in Europe, giving people more opportunities to send signals concerning their political affiliation."

Nevertheless, the researchers don't foresee the impact of the partisan divide waning anytime soon in democracies. In fact, Iyengar's past research shows the rift among opposing parties has widened over the past 30 years.

"Defined in terms of affect, voters' sense of partisanship seems to represent a dominant divide in modern democracies and the strongest basis for group polarization," the researchers write.

9

Social Psychology Can Bridge the Partisan Divide

Lee De-Wit, Cameron Brick, and Sander Van Der Linden

Lee De-Wit, PhD, is a lecturer in political psychology at Cambridge University. Sander Van Der Linden, PhD, is assistant professor of social psychology and director of the Cambridge Social Decision-Making Lab at the University of Cambridge. Cameron Brick, PhD, is a social psychologist and research associate at the University of Cambridge, U.K.

Even when people agree on specific issues, they tend to prefer policies proposed by members of their political party and oppose those generated by the other party. In this "us versus them" political environment, new policies, regardless of their merit, can quickly become a source of conflict over which political parties clash. Social psychology suggests that polarization is being made worse by underlying psychological processes that form how people interpret identity and groups. Therefore, social psychology offers some insights into potential ways to reduce political polarization. Ideas such as fostering perspective-taking, making changes to voting systems, and developing shared goals may bring Americans back together.

"What Are the Solutions to Political Polarization?" by Lee De-Wit, Cameron Brick, and Sander Van Der Linden, The Greater Good Science Center at the University of California, Berkeley, July 2, 2019. This article originally appeared on *Greater Good*, the online magazine of the Greater Good Science Center at UC Berkeley. Reprinted by permission.

What drives political polarization?

Is it simply disagreement over the great issues of the day? Not necessarily. Recent research by the More in Common Foundation found that more than three-fourths of Americans support both stricter gun laws and a pathway to citizenship for undocumented immigrants brought here as children. Roughly the same number of Americans agree "that our differences are not so great that we cannot come together."

Are they right?

The More in Common results could be interpreted to suggest that we can build bipartisan support for specific policies by focusing more on their boring nuts and bolts. Unfortunately, however, voters don't evaluate policies in isolation. Research has highlighted that people actively use partisan cues when evaluating different policies.

For example, a study by Carlee Beth Hawkins and Brian Nosek shows that labeling policies as "Democrat" or "Republican" can influence policy support, depending on the implicit bias of participants toward each party. A 2017 study by David Tannenbaum and colleagues finds that support for policy "nudges"—such as changing 401k retirement accounts to opt-out rather than opt-in—was heavily influenced by whether they were framed as supporting the goals of the Democratic or Republican party. This was true of regular US citizens and for senior government leaders. Similarly, a 2018 study by Leaf Van Boven and colleagues finds that the majority of Republicans agree that climate change is happening—but their support for policy solutions declined when presented by Democrats.

In other words, people like policies proposed by members of their own in-group—and they don't like ideas generated by out-groups. This dynamic is not new. Since the 1950s, social psychologists have tried to understand what pits groups against each other—and today, they're applying these insights to figure out what is happening in the United States. This research doesn't provide definitive answers, but it does suggest some potential solutions, from changes to the voting system to the development of common goals that might enable groups to work together.

How Morality Becomes Partisan

The More in Common report illustrates that some of the most divisive topics often involve deep moral beliefs. For example, different political groups are very polarized on beliefs about responsibility, such as "people's outcomes in life are determined largely by forces outside of their control," or "people are largely responsible for their own outcomes in life." Similarly, liberals and conservatives are very divided on questions of whether parenting should focus on cultivating a child's curiosity versus good manners, or independence versus respect for elders.

In a new study published this year, Annemarie S. Walter and David P. Redlawsk directly pitted people's moral concerns with their partisan identity. They presented 2,000 participants with examples of different moral violations by different actors. Based on previous research, Walter and Redlawsk had thought that the nature of the moral violation might be the most significant factor in people's evaluations, as there are reasons to think that liberals and conservatives are concerned with some moral violations more than others. What they found, however, is that it *wasn't* the nature of the moral violation that was most important. Instead, it was the political allegiance of the violator. Democrats in the study were prone to giving Democrats a pass; the same was even more true of Republicans.

This partisan influence on policy preferences and moral judgements is a cause for both hope and concern. On one hand, it reiterates a point made by Daniel Yudkin in a *New York Times* op-ed about the More in Common report: that the US may actually be less politically polarized based on certain moral or policy issues—at least when there aren't clear partisan associations. On the other hand, it highlights that as soon as a moral or political issue becomes associated with a particular party, it can become polarizing.

This is why it increasingly feels like US politics has entered into a vicious cycle, whereby the moral and emotional language used to galvanize one side is directly antagonizing the other. The us-and-them nature of the debate has led to such a breakdown of trust that even hearing a policy proposed by the other side can be enough to trigger opposition to that policy. New policies (whatever their merit) can therefore quickly become symbols of conflict for the two sides to rally around.

What Are the Solutions?

This suggests that while there might be various political seeds that have helped drive the recent spike in polarization, it has gotten to a point where polarization is being exacerbated by some of the psychological processes that shape how we interpret identity and groups. This is a significant point to understand because it highlights that if we are to address polarization, we need to think not just about political solutions, but also solutions that are grounded in our understanding of social psychology.

1. Intergroup Contact

The "contact hypothesis" suggests that getting to know each other can reduce prejudice between groups. However, social contact can be done well and done badly. As we discussed in a previous article, following political opponents on Twitter can make people more extreme in their political views. It turns out that many conditions have to be met for contact to reduce prejudice, including having contact be sustained, with more than one member of the group, including a genuine exchange of ideas, and between individuals of similar social rank. These conditions have been very difficult to meet in designing social policies.

One promising civic model for enabling more meaningful contact between groups in conflict involves "Citizens Assemblies," where representative citizens are brought together to deliberate over challenging social or political issues. These assemblies can be thought of as a kind of jury duty for political deliberation, and they offer a platform for different groups to discuss issues in a way that can highlight where common ground exists and how it can be acted upon.

For example, Ireland has run several Citizens Assembles since 2016 that made policy recommendations that have been credited with advances in Ireland's approach to climate change. Indeed, participants in a recent Citizens Assembly on Brexit, run by Alan Renwick and colleagues at University College London, came to a compromise that could resolve the current impasse surrounding the U.K.'s decision to leave the European Union.

2. Perspective Taking

Perhaps one of the most important aspects of contact is that it might enable one to see things from another's perspective. The promise of perspective taking was recently illustrated in an experiment to attempt to change support for issues faced by transgender minorities. In this intervention, a brief exchange exploring a range of issues from the perspective of a trans individual was sufficient to shift people's attitudes on this controversial topic. Indeed, the attitude change seemed to persist even six months later, which is unusual for brief psychological interventions.

In his book *The Better Angels of Our Nature*, Pinker argues that the printing press may have had an important role in increasing levels of empathy following the Enlightenment by making it easier to read stories framed in the perspective of others. Indeed, Pinker speculates that some of the literature written from the perspective of black slaves may have been instrumental to the abolition of slavery.

Considering the revolution in communication technology in our lifetimes, social media may have done more to promote taking sides than seeing the world through the eyes of another. Social media companies, and the governments that regulate them, clearly need to reflect on the extent to which these platforms encourage "side taking" instead of "perspective taking."

3. Superordinate Goals

One of the clearest solutions from the psychological literature is that identity-based conflicts require common goals or a "superordinate" sense of identity to bring people back together. In other words, we need a large sense of ourselves that is able to bridge smaller differences. This need to create a superordinate identity has clearly been intuitive to rulers for centuries, who would use various traditions and ceremonies to help build alliances between different countries and cultures.

Of course, superordinate goals also come with a potential risk. Whenever we form an in-group, we also create out-groups. As Richard Dawkins recently tweeted:

> *National pride has evil consequences. Prefer pride in humanity. German pride gave us Hitler, American pride gave us Trump, British pride gave us Brexit. If you must have pride, be proud that Homo sapiens could produce a Darwin, Shakespeare, Mandela, Einstein, Beethoven.*

Unfortunately, drawing a parallel between Trump and Hitler is perhaps itself an illustration of the polarized nature of modern discourse. Dawkins does have a point, however: The use of a superordinate identity such as American or European has potential risks. So, should we just think of ourselves as humans—or is the idea of "humanity" too abstract? Former British prime minister Theresa May famously criticized such a universalist perspective, stating: "If you believe you are a citizen of the world, you are a citizen of nowhere."

Is that true? Research suggests that a universalist perspective might well have underappreciated benefits. Sam McFarland and colleagues recently reviewed this topic and found that those who identify highly as citizens of the world are indeed more empathic. Of course, those who are more empathic might simply identify more as international citizens. This idea warrants further testing, particularly as McFarland and colleagues identify several factors that might serve to further develop this sense of international citizenship.

4. Proportional Voting

While searching for psychological solutions to polarization, it's important not to ignore the context in which political decisions are made, and to think about the way in which different political systems will engage with, and exacerbate, aspects of our psychology.

The US is one of the few countries to be dominated by just two political parties. This fact is almost certainly a reflection of the "winner take all"/"first past the post" voting system. Many countries employ a proportional (or mixed) system, which means that if a party gets 5 percent of the popular vote, they will receive 5 percent of the seats in a given representative body. In the US, this party would almost certainly get no representation—which could worsen the us-and-them dynamic of the US political system.

For now, however, there isn't systematic evidence comparing the extent of identity-based politics with the political system used in the US. Unfortunately, that kind of large-scale, cross-country research is often the most difficult to obtain, but could be exactly what we need to understand how different voting systems might influence polarization.

That said, there is evidence that more proportional systems have higher levels of voter turnout (at least for supporters of smaller parties). In turn, that increase in turnout is correlated with citizens being more likely to report feeling that their vote makes a difference. This doesn't necessarily stop politics becoming less polarized, but it might make it harder for the extremes to come to dominate.

5. Voting for Policies, Not for Parties

Another potential solution to identity-based policy preferences is to hold direct referendums on specific issues. Among large territories, California and Switzerland both regularly use referendums to address complex policy topics. Referendums are used less frequently in other countries to try to resolve controversial topics, as was the case with gay marriage in Australia or voting reform in New Zealand. When designed well, referendums might cut across existing partisan divides, and if a clear majority is reached, they can signal a new social norm that can help a country move forward.

For those who are familiar with the fallout from the recent Brexit referendum in the U.K., however, this suggestion would probably seem a little laughable. Contemptuous, even. Indeed, there is evidence that the referendum in the U.K. has itself spilled over into a new form of emotional polarization, as recent data from YouGov highlights that (especially younger) "Remain" supporters would not want to see a close relative marry a "Leaver" (a member of the opposing political camp). There's another problem as well: While Australians did indeed vote to legalize same-sex marriage, it could have gone the other way; allowing the majority to vote on the civil and human rights of a minority is very risky.

Like many complex political systems, however, referendums can be designed well and designed badly. In countries with more established systems of direct democracy, the U.K. referendum wouldn't have even been legal. For example, in Switzerland, referendums have to be about precisely defined changes to the law, not vaguely defined outcomes. In New Zealand's referendum on the voting system, an independent educational body was created to inform both sides of the debate without taking a position (as the British government controversially did during the Brexit referendum).

The psychological impact of more direct voting systems is worthy of further enquiry. When poorly implemented, referendums risk causing new fault lines along which polarization can manifest. When well implemented, referendums might cut across existing lines of polarization and help establish a new social norm that can move a country forward.

From reframing issues to tap into a superordinate sense of identity, to promoting forms of contact that encourage perspective taking, social psychology does offer some useful ideas for thinking about how to tackle polarization. Furthermore, social psychology provides insights into the potential implications of different kinds of voting systems and the way in which they might exacerbate or diminish identity-based politics. As we have been careful to try and illustrate, however, experiments in social psychology do not yield off-the-shelf solutions that would be effective in all political contexts. Nevertheless, the farther that modern politics sinks into a self-fulfilling cycle of identity-based polarization, the more we'll need new insights from social science.

10

Negative Partisanship Causes Votes Along Party Lines

Charlie Cook

Charlie Cook is an American political analyst who specializes in election forecasts and political trends.

As partisanship rises in US politics, negative partisanship is also surging. Negative partisanship causes people who identify with one political party to be motivated more by their dislike for the opposition party or candidate than their support for their party. Negative partisanship leads citizens to vote against a candidate and party rather than voting for one whose policies they support. In the 2018 midterm elections, voters increasingly chose Senate and House of Representative candidates based on their party, not their policies.

It's no secret that the level of political acrimony in the 1970s and 1980s now pales in comparison to the current climate of partisanship. Indeed, when the Justice Department on Thursday releases Special Counsel Robert Mueller's partially redacted report on Russian interference in the 2016 presidential election, reactions will inevitably fall along partisan lines.

There's something more specific at play, however. Partisanship used to be thought of as something practiced primarily by super-believers, and in some cases that's still true. But now we are seeing a rise in what's known as negative partisanship, in which partisan

"The Power of 'Negative Partisanship,'" by Charlie Cook, Cook Political Report, April 19, 2019. Reprinted by permission.

zealots are not enamored with their own party or candidates as much as they loathe anyone in the opposition party.

As Emory University political scientists Alan Abramowitz and Steven Webster observe: "To a greater extent than at any time in the post–World War II era, the outcomes of elections below the presidential level reflect the outcomes of presidential elections. As a result, the famous comment by the late Tip O'Neill that 'all politics is local' now seems rather quaint. In the 21st century United States, it increasingly appears that all politics is national."

In "The Strengthening of Partisan Affect," Stanford political scientists Shanto Iyengar and Masha Krupenkin note that "as animosity toward the opposing party has intensified, it has taken on a new role as the prime motivator in partisans' political lives." Iyengar and Krupenkin go on to suggest that "the impact of feelings toward the out-party on both vote choice and the decision to participate has increased since 2000; today it is out-group animus rather than in-group favoritism that drives political behavior."

For years my unfortunate suspicion has been that the strongest emotion in politics is not love but hate, that opposition unites, that more passion is often found among those con than pro. The title of another piece written by Abramowitz and Webster says it all: "Negative Partisanship: Why Americans Dislike Parties But Behave Like Rabid Partisans."

This came into play in last year's midterm elections in a big way. University of California (San Diego) political scientist Gary Jacobson, in a paper presented this month to the Midwest Political Science Association, argued that while in many ways the 2018 elections behaved much like the pattern we've come to expect in midterms, in its particulars the 2018 vote "was anything but ordinary." A crucial oddity was the disjunction between presidential approval and the economy. Ordinarily, a president enjoying very good economic numbers (solid economic growth, very low unemployment, low inflation, a strong stock market, and the rosiest public views of the economy in more than two decades) during a time of relative peace would be expected to have much higher overall approval ratings than Trump was receiving.

But this election, Jacobson suggests, was far more about Trump and partisanship than about the economy, with partisans holding in line more than they have since the 1940s and '50s. Trump garnered approval ratings among Republicans in the vicinity of 90 percent but in the single digits among Democrats. Jacobson writes: "The stability of popular opinions of Trump is no mystery, for his conduct as president has given most people no reason to revise what they thought of him as a candidate. Democrats and others appalled by his character and objectives before the election have seen their worst expectations confirmed. Trump has mounted a root-and-branch assault on Barack Obama's entire legacy (on health care, environmental protection, financial regulation, taxes, fiscal policy, immigration, and foreign trade)."

Looking over at the GOP, Jacobson suggests that "Trump has also largely met the expectations of the Republicans who voted for him, and they, like Democrats, also continue to regard him pretty much as they did before he was elected. Virtually everything he has said or done as president has catered exclusively to the coalition that elected him, its white-nationalist segment in particular, but also small-government and religious conservatives." They enjoy his responses to critics, his disdain of the mainstream media, and applaud his rhetoric.

Operationally, we see this in House and Senate races. Jacobson points out in his MPSA paper that five of the six Senate seats that changed parties in 2018 went for the party that won the state in 2016. Now, 89 of 100 senators now represent a state won by their respective party's presidential nominee in the last election, an all-time high.

Looking over at the House side, in 2015, Jacobson wrote in *The Journal of Politics* that "the changing effects of partisanship are also manifest in the incidence of ticket splitting." Ticket splitting between House and presidential races doubled between the 1950s and 1970s, but gradually declined to the extent that in 2012 it was the smallest for any election in the entire series." This pattern continued in the 2016 election.

The old saying that "I vote the person not the party," once a commonplace belief, is now just a cliché. As such, it is getting harder and harder for incumbents or challengers to swim upstream. When they do, it is often because that state or district is in a transition period as it shifts from blue to red, or vice versa.

As for voters, expect them to continue taking it out on the party they hate. Their own party's candidates are a secondary concern.

11

Under Negative Partisanship, Fear Motivates Voters

Eric Black

Eric Black is an award-winning journalist who writes about national and state politics, policy, government, and history.

Research shows that US voters are increasingly motivated by their dislike and fear of the opposition political party than support for their party. This concept, called negative partisanship, presents a danger to democracy. Fear is a powerful motivator that drives voter turnout. Recognizing this phenomenon, candidates no longer need to inspire voters with their ideas. Instead, they can encourage fear and anger toward the opposing party to win elections. Because of negative partisanship, the out-of-power party often has an election turnout advantage, as fearful voters flock to the polls.

The voter turnout on Tuesday in Minnesota was the highest of any Minnesota primary in more than 20 years (although primary turnouts are always lower than general elections). The turnout on the Democratic side was roughly double the Republican side. To overstate the obvious, if Democrats double Republican turnout in November, the Dems will win everything.

But that's just an "if." You could torture those numbers too much, especially if you are trying to use them to see what's going to happen next. Considering that in the 2016 general election,

"Exploring the Concept of Negative Partisanship—and How It Might Affect November's Results," by Eric Black, MinnPost, August 16, 2018. Reprinted by permission.

almost every fool who tried tell us what would happen predicted that Hillary Clinton would beat Donald Trump, I suggest we all get out of the habit of demanding to know what's going to happen, and that people in the pundit class develop a serious case of humility about their ability to see the future.

But, despite all of that well-founded humility, I do want to encourage you to think about a somewhat fashionable concept in political science, which will inevitably lead to the temptation to think about the future.

The concept has been called "negative partisanship." Negative partisanship refers to those voters who are more motivated to vote by their fears of the bad things the opposition party will do than they are by the good things they hope their own party will do. (In 1992, the Democratic presidential ticket put out a button urging voters to vote their hopes, not their fears. Negative partisanship is roughly the opposite. It is voting one's fears.)

Survey data makes quite clear that more and more voters are more and more motivated by their dislike and fear of the other party than by their enthusiasm for their own ticket.

Political scientist Alan Abramowitz of Emory University has been a leader in developing and presenting the arguments that over recent cycles the electorate has been steadily more motivated by their fears of what the other party will do than their enthusiasm for what their own party will do.

"Our research shows that Americans increasingly are voting against the opposing party more than they are voting for their own party," Abramowitz wrote last year in Politico.

The data are quite convincing. In a more scholarly article, Abramowitz cited numbers from the American National Election Studies, which has surveyed voters for more than 70 years, and which has asked voters since 1978 to rate the warmth of their feelings for both major parties on a "feelings thermometer."

The average positivity of those feelings has gone down steadily and, in 2016, the percentage of respondents who said they had a favorable opinion of both parties hit a record low. The average positive rating by respondents toward their own party has gone down fairly steadily over the years, but the average rating for the "other" party has gone down much, much more. That created a big gap, but also led Abramowitz to argue that voters are less motivated by enthusiasm for their own party and more motivated by feelings bordering on fear and hatred for the other.

In an effort to explain the concept to a non-scholarly audience, Abramowitz wrote in Politico:

> *Our research shows that Americans increasingly are voting against the opposing party more than they are voting for their own party. …*
>
> *There's a longer-term danger to our democratic system here, that is likely to survive well beyond Trump. In today's environment, rather than seeking to inspire voters around a cohesive and forward-looking vision, politicians need only incite fear and anger toward the opposing party to win and maintain power. Until that fundamental incentive goes away, expect politics to get even uglier.*

And then, in a tortured sports metaphor that doesn't really work for me (unless we're talking about the New York Yankees), Abramowitz wrote:

> *The concept is pretty simple: Over the past few decades, American politics has become like a bitter sports rivalry, in which the parties hang together mainly out of sheer hatred of the other team, rather than a shared sense of purpose. Republicans might not love the president, but they absolutely loathe his Democratic adversaries. And it's also true of Democrats, who might be consumed by their internal feuds over foreign policy and the proper role of government were it not for Trump.*
>
> *Negative partisanship explains nearly everything in American politics today—from why Trump's base is unlikely to abandon him even if, as he once said, he were to shoot someone on Fifth Avenue, to why it was so easy for vulnerable red-state Democrats to resist defecting on the health care bill.*
>
> *Consider, for instance, that while Trump's approval ratings have lately been in the mid- to upper 30s, he has maintained support of the overwhelming majority of Republican voters—around 80 percent in Gallup's tracking poll. And that's what*

matters to him and to most Republican members of Congress. The president understands that as long as that Republican base remains loyal to him, he is unlikely to face a serious challenge from GOP members of the House and Senate. He also knows that the surest way to keep the support of his base is by attacking Democrats, especially the two most prominent leaders of the Democratic Party—Hillary Clinton and Barack Obama. What looks like an unhealthy Twitter obsession over "Crooked Hillary" and her emails is more likely a team-building exercise—a shrewd effort to keep his party focused on their shared enemy: Democrats. And so far, it's working for him.

This is a long way from my growing up years in the 1950s, when even Democrats "liked Ike." Although it's alarming, it resonates for me. But, with apologies for writing too long, let me finish with the thoughts of another political scientist who builds on Abramowitz.

Rachel Bitcofer, who seems to work on election projections for the Wason Center for Public Policy, endorses negative partisanship as a way of explaining why many voters turn out, but adds that voters are even more motivated to turn out if the party they favor is out of power, because the experience of having the opposing party in power adds to their motivation.

It kind of makes sense to me. In an essay titled "Signs, Signs, Everywhere Are Signs: Why Democrats Will Win Big in the 2018 Midterms," she adds:

Out of power partisans vote because fear is an excellent motivator. Especially the kind of fear that comes from seeing the opposition party enacting policies you don't support and stacking the federal courts with judges with the "wrong" ideology.

Republican success in recent national elections fed on a desperate backlash among Republicans at seeing Obama in power. She writes:

For Republicans, elections in the Obama era, both big and small, were framed as a referendum on Barack Obama and Nancy Pelosi. This brilliant messaging, combined with a complacent Democratic electorate, allowed Republicans to over perform their share of the electorate by 5 points in the 2010 midterms and 10 points in 2014 in midterms. It is negative partisanship among opposition party voters that drives the midterm effect, not movement of independent voters back and forth between the parties.

Because of negative partisanship Democrats will have a significant enthusiasm advantage in turnout in elections so long as Donald Trump sits in the White House. In places where there are large pools of untapped Democratic voters, the party is going to win marginal seats as well as some seats that have not been competitive since at least 2006.

That, she says, explains Democratic success in several special elections in districts that Trump carried by wide margins in 2018. Bitcofer adds:

My analysis of special elections since Trump was elected reveals that Democratic Party candidates are over-performing Hillary Clinton's share of the two-party vote by an average of 7.36 points while Republican Party candidates have under-performed Trump's vote share by an average of -3.47 for a net improvement advantage for Democrats of 10.83 points.

12

Negative Partisanship Increasingly Dominates Elections

Harry Zahn

Harry Zahn is a multimedia journalist at the PBS NewsHour *with a special interest in politics, writing broadcast copy, producing interviews, and authoring articles for print and online publication.*

Increasingly, American politics and elections are dominated by negative partisanship. Democratic and Republican voters are motivated by negative feelings toward the opposition party and its candidates. An increasing number of Americans believe the opposing party's policies threaten America's well-being. Many political observers predict that political polarization will grow worse over time. They identify partisan media sources and associations with people who share similar political views as two factors driving negative partisanship. Some experts believe that negative partisanship will eventually decline as policies and candidates move to bridge the party divide.

There were the "Lock her up!" chants that rang through Donald Trump's campaign rallies, encouraged by the President-elect himself. There was Hillary Clinton's famous "basket of deplorables" comment and her warning to a reporter: "I'm the last thing standing between you and the apocalypse." The mudslinging from both sides

"Why 'Negative Partisanship' Is Flipping Politics on Its Head," by Harry Zahn, PBS NewsHour Website, December 23, 2016.

reached new lows in an election pitting the two most unpopular presidential candidates in modern history.

But the negativity on display in the 2016 election—from the candidates, their surrogates and the public alike—also exposed a trend in American politics that predates Clinton and Trump's brutal showdown.

Increasingly, Democratic and Republican voters are motivated by negative feelings toward the other party and its candidates, according to political scientists Alan Abramowitz and Steven Webster, authors of the 2015 study, "The rise of negative partisanship and the nationalization of US elections in the 21st century."

The most critical question in any US election used to be, "Who are you voting for?" In 2016, it might as well have been: "Who are you voting against?"

In interviews, Abramowitz and other political scientists and experts said the kind of voter antagonism directed toward Clinton and Trump could become the norm, not the exception, in future elections.

Negative partisanship is "very real. We have pretty good evidence for that," said Barry Burden, the director of the Elections Research Center at the University of Wisconsin–Madison. "And it's gotten more severe over time."

Negative Views on the Rise Since 1980

The rise of negative partisanship is backed up by troves of data from the past three-plus decades. Abramowitz and Webster's analysis of data from the American National Election Studies (ANES), the largest national voter survey, found a sharp increase in voters' party loyalty in federal elections since 1980, as well as a boost in straight-ticket voting.

From 1980 to 2012, the ANES data also shows that voters' ratings of their own parties dipped from 72 degrees to 70 degrees (respondents rate their feelings toward a party on a feeling thermometer; 100 is extremely positive, 0 is extremely negative, and 50 is neutral).

But over that same 32-year span—which stretches from the presidency of Ronald Reagan to that of President Obama—voters' attitudes about the opposing party deteriorated. In 1980, voters' average rating of the opposing party was 45 degrees. By 2012, the average had fallen to 30 degrees.

The ANES data is supported by other studies documenting the rise of negative partisanship.

Pew data, for example, shows a rise in the percentage of voters in each party who consider the other party "unfavorable." At the same time, Pew found an even swifter uptick in the number of voters who find the other party "very unfavorable."

In 1994, 21 percent of Republicans held a "very unfavorable" view of the Democratic Party, a 2016 Pew study found. That number jumped to 32 percent in 2008 and 58 percent this year.

Democratic voters have followed a similar pattern, according to Pew. In 1994, 17 percent held a "very unfavorable" view of the Republican Party. That percentage climbed to 37 percent in 2008, and 55 percent in 2016.

So, the animosity is mutual. And it's growing.

Perhaps it's no surprise, then, that Republicans and Democrats believe the other side is putting the country in jeopardy. Pew found that in 2016, 45 percent of Republicans and 41 percent of Democrats believe the opposing party's policies are a threat to the nation's well-being—up from 36 and 27 percent, respectively, in 2014.

Both campaigns seized on these views in the presidential race, Abramowitz said in an interview.

"Demonizing Hillary Clinton was a key to the success of the Republican strategy," Abramowitz said, and among Democrats, "there was very strong dislike for Donald Trump."

Though much of the political science community believes negative partisanship is on the rise, not everyone saw it as the driving force behind the 2016 election. Lara Brown, a professor of political science at George Washington University, said Donald Trump played to pent-up voter frustration with establishment leaders across the political spectrum.

"To a certain extent, people were voting for Donald Trump, because he was against both parties," Brown said. "I see Donald Trump much more as a reaction to the fact that, basically since 2005, [many voters believe that] both parties have betrayed the American public. They promised a lot, and they haven't really delivered."

Abramowitz acknowledged Trump's unique appeal as an outsider candidate. But he noted that most incumbents, including many vulnerable Republican senators, won reelection in 2016, further proof of the recent spike in party loyalty and straight-ticket voting.

"What was kind of remarkable in this election was that while Trump was having all this success attacking the establishment and running as this very unconventional candidate," voters still opted for establishment candidates in congressional races, Abramowitz said.

Only two incumbents lost reelection in the Senate in a year with 34 seats up for grabs. In the House, 380 out of the 393 incumbents who ran for reelection won a new term.

Root Causes of Negative Partisanship

The rise in negative partisanship since the Reagan era has several root causes. But Abramowitz said the trend mainly stems from changes in both parties' voter bases, as well as divisions over race, religion and the role of government.

"There's a growing racial divide between the parties, both in terms of race and racial attitudes," Abramowitz said. "Social attitudes and cultural values [played a role, along with] a great big division over how one views the government and the role of government."

Of course, these divisions aren't new. Partisanship and political polarization have been part of US politics since the dawn of the republic.

Supporters of the Federalist and the Democratic-Republican parties, along with their standard bearers—Alexander Hamilton and Thomas Jefferson—had a contentious relationship in the late 18th and early 19th centuries.

More recently, political polarization spiked during the 1960s, when white Southern Democratic voters and politicians left the party in droves for the GOP in response to the civil rights movement.

"That wiped out a lot of moderate Southern Democrats, [and] it replaced them with very conservative Republicans," said Allan Lichtman, a historian at American University who has famously predicted every presidential election for the past 30 years. The resulting shakeup pushed the "Democratic Party to the left and the Republican Party to the right."

One of the main differences between then and now, is the proliferation of partisan media outlets that reinforce voters' opinions. The abundance of right and left-leaning news (and fake news), coupled with the growing influence of money in politics, has transformed elections at every level into partisan slugfests.

"Voters no longer view House, Senate and local elections as separate arenas of competition from presidential elections. On the contrary, voters now view their choices in elections at all levels through the lens of negative partisanship," Abramowitz and Webster wrote in their 2015 study.

They added: "At all levels of government, the greatest concern of party supporters is preventing the opposing party from gaining power. For this reason, negative partisanship has nationalized American elections."

These changes help explain why, in the end, so many anti-Trump Republicans supported a highly unusual and controversial candidate who held stances on issues like infrastructure and trade that are not aligned with modern Republican orthodoxy. On the other side, many liberal Bernie Sanders supporters who backed Clinton in the general election were more motivated by a desire to stop Trump than by enthusiasm for the party's nominee.

Many political observers said the nation's political polarization will only worsen with time.

"It is difficult to identify ways that negative partisanship might be dampened," said Burden, the head of the University of Wisconsin–Madison's elections center. "As long as people continue to consume partisan media sources and associate with people with similar attitudes, there are not many opportunities to see good aspects in the other side."

But some were more optimistic.

"I'm not convinced that [negative partisanship] is as enduring as what some might argue," said Jan Leighley, a political science professor at American University. "I think there are probably policies, candidates, periods, in which the right elite 'move,' if you will, can bridge that polarization."

13

The Influence of Partisan News Is Real but Limited

Peter Dizikes

Peter Dizikes is the social sciences, business, and humanities writer at the MIT News Office.

The expansion of TV news from three broadcast networks to include several major cable news networks has led to a more partisan experience for those who choose it. But how much does this partisan news coverage affect the viewing public? Research suggests that such exposure can have differing effects depending on the type of person. Those who already exhibit a preference for partisan news appear to be less influenced than those people who are relatively nonpolitical. In general, however, most people in the United States are not interested in political news.

It's a classic question in contemporary politics: Does partisan news media coverage shape people's ideologies? Or do people decide to consume political media that is already aligned with their beliefs?

A new study led by MIT political scientists tackles this issue head-on and arrives at a nuanced conclusion: While partisan media does indeed have "a strong persuasive impact" on political attitudes, as the researchers write in a newly published paper, news media exposure has a bigger impact on people without strongly

"Does Cable News Shape Your Views?" by Peter Dizikes, Massachusetts Institute of Technology (MIT), August 7, 2019. Reprinted by permission.

held preferences for partisan media than it does for people who seek out partisan media outlets.

In short, certain kinds of political media affect a cross-section of viewers in varying manners, and to varying degrees—so while the influence of partisan news is real, it also has its limits.

"Different populations are going to respond to partisan media in different ways," says Adam Berinsky, the Mitsui Professor of Political Science and director of the Political Experiments Research Lab (PERL) at MIT, and a co-author of the study.

"Political persuasion is hard," Berinsky adds. "If it were easy, the world would already look a lot different."

The paper, "Persuading the Enemy: Estimating the Persuasive Effects of Partisan Media with the Preference-Incorporating Choice and Assignment Design," is now available in advance online form from the *American Political Science Review*.

In addition to Berinsky, the authors are Justin de Benedictis-Kessner, PhD '17, an assistant professor of political science at Boston University; Mathew A. Baum, a professor at the Harvard Kennedy School; and Teppei Yamamoto, an associate professor in MIT's Department of Political Science.

Breaking Down the Problem

Substantial political science literature has debated the question of media influence; some scholars have contended that partisan media significantly shapes public opinion, but others have argued that "selective exposure," in which people watch what they already agree with, is predominant.

"It's a really tricky problem," Berinsky says. "How do you disentangle these things?"

The new research aims to do that, in part, by disaggregating the viewing public. The study consists of a series of experiments and surveys analyzing the responses of smaller subgroups, which were divided according to media consumption preferences, ideology, and more.

That allows the researchers to tease apart the cause-and-effect issues surrounding media consumption by looking more specifically at the impact of media on people with different ideologies and different levels of willingness to view media. The researchers call this approach the Preference-Incorporating Choice and Assignment design, or PICA.

For instance, one experiment within the study gave participants the option of reading web posts from either the conservative Fox News channel; MSNBC, which has several shows leaning in a significantly more liberal-left direction; or the Food Network. Other participants were assigned to watch one of the three.

By examining viewer responses to the content, the scholars found that people who elected to read materials from partisan news channels were less influenced by the content. By contrast, participants who gravitated to the Food Network but were assigned to watch cable news, were more influenced by the content.

How big is the effect? Quantitatively, the researchers found, a single exposure to partisan media can change the views of relatively nonpolitical citizens by an amount equal to one-third of the average ideological gap that exists between partisans on the right and left sides of the political spectrum.

Thus, the influence of cable news depends on who it is reaching. "People do respond differently based on their preferences," Berinsky says.

And while the impact of partisan cable news on people who elect to watch it is smaller, it does exist, the researchers found. For instance, in another of the study's experiments, the researchers tested cable news' effects on viewers' beliefs about marijuana legislation. Even among regular cable-news viewers, partisan content influenced people's views.

Overall, Yamamoto states, the PICA method is novel because it "allows us to make inferences about what is never [otherwise] directly observable," that is, the impact of partisan media on people who would normally choose not to consume it.

"Most People Just Don't Want News"

To put the findings in the context of daily news viewership in the US, consider the recent congressional hearings in which special counsel Robert Mueller testified about his presidential investigation. Fox News led the cable ratings with an average of 3 million viewers during most of the day, while MSNBC had an average of 2.4 million viewers. Overall, 13 million people watched. But the Super Bowl, for example, regularly pulls in around 100 million viewers.

"Most people just don't want to be exposed to political news," Berinsky notes. "These are not bad people or bad citizens. In theory, a democracy is working well when you can ignore politics."

One implication of the larger lack of interest in politics, consequently, is that any audience gains that partisan media outlets experience can produce relatively greater influence—since that growth would apply to formerly irregular consumers of news, who may be more easily influenced. Again, though, such audience gains are likely to be limited, due to the reluctance of most Americans to consume partisan media.

"We only learned those people are persuadable because we made them watch the news," Berinsky says.

Other scholars in the field say the paper is a valuable addition to the literature on media influence. Kevin Arceneaux, the Thomas J. Freaney, Jr. Professor of Political Science and director of the Behavioral Foundations Lab at Temple University, says the study "represents an important methodological leap forward in the study of media effects."

Arceneaux says the researchers "convincingly demonstrate that partisan news media have the largest effects among individuals who tend to avoid consuming news," and suggests some possible implications pertaining to the larger media landscape.

For people who do follow politics, he suggests, having many news options available may "blunt the persuasive and polarizing effects of partisan news media"; at the same time, social media could be "an important source of polarization" by introducing some people to news. Arceneaux also notes that further research on the effects of "counterattitudinal" partisan news—content that argues against the beliefs of consumers—would shed more light on the dynamics of media influence.

14

Partisan Media Is Fueled by Lack of Trust in Mainstream News

Matt Grossmann

Matt Grossmann is the director of the Institute for Public Policy and Social Research (IPPSR) and professor of political science at Michigan State University.

Media bias has a long history in the United States. Partisan newspapers were common in the nineteenth century. In the early twentieth century, the American Society of Newspaper Editors added impartiality to its journalist code of ethics and called for news reports to be free of bias or opinion. Even so, Republicans remained skeptical of the mostly Democratic media's ability to maintain independence and equally represent their views. Perception of mainstream media bias, both real and perceived, has driven the public's lack of trust in mainstream journalism and the rise of partisan media outlets. As a result, the twentieth-century phenomenon of trusted, unbiased media may fade away.

In the age of Fox News Channel, talk radio, and MSNBC, it is tempting to think we have entered an unprecedented age of biased media. But partisan bias is actually the norm in media history. As Jonathan Ladd argues, "The existence of an independent, powerful, widely respected news media establishment

"Media Bias (Real and Perceived) and the Rise of Partisan Media," by Matt Grossmann, Niskanen Center, November 6, 2017. Reprinted by permission.

is an historical anomaly. Prior to the twentieth century, such an institution had never existed in American history."

In the nineteenth century, overtly partisan newspapers were the norm. Independent journalism was a successful countervailing movement that brought with it standards of unbiased political coverage. Joseph Pulitzer, the Democratic politician and newspaperman, helped establish the Columbia School of Journalism in 1912 and the Pulitzer Prizes in 1917. The American Society of Newspaper Editors codified an impartiality principle in its 1923 code of ethics: "News reports should be free from opinion or bias of any kind."

But Republicans have long been skeptical of the ability of an independent press to equally represent their views. Donald Trump's declaration of any contrary coverage as "fake news" is a more extreme version of a long-standing complaint. As Ladd finds, "criticism of the institutional news media was a defining characteristic" of the conservative movement and Barry Goldwater's nomination campaign. His supporters later founded the Committee to Combat Bias in Broadcasting and Accuracy in Media to monitor the news for bias. Complaints about media bias were common in subsequent Republican administrations and eventually came to dominate Republican campaigns. One study found that 92% of claims of media bias in the 1988, 1992, and 1996 elections came from Republicans alleging liberal bias.

These complaints were directly tied to the rise of explicitly conservative media as alternatives to mainstream news. Kathleen Hall Jamieson and Joseph Capella, who studied the Rush Limbaugh show for a full year, found that he mentioned media bias every single day. Fox News Channel was created to counter perceived liberal bias, calling itself "fair and balanced" with the motto "we report, you decide."

Conservative skepticism of the ability of an independent press to be unbiased was a reaction to the basic demographics of journalism. Reporters have been and remain disproportionately Democrats and liberals (compared to the general public). Lars

Willnat and David Weaver found that the proportion of Republican reporters dropped from an already-low 26% in 1971 to 7% in 2013. Republicans and conservatives are more common in local television news, but are rarely seen at national mainstream news outlets.

Are the Mainstream Media Biased in Favor of Democrats and Liberalism?

Even if reporters are disproportionately Democrats and liberals, they may be able to produce unbiased news by pursuing objective evidence or balanced coverage. Do they succeed?

Overall, studies examining the content of news coverage have not found consistent evidence of bias favoring Democrats or Republicans across many different elections. There are studies finding Republican bias and studies finding Democratic bias. Others find only media bias toward the frontrunner, regardless of party. Dave D'Alessio examined 99 prior studies of presidential election coverage bias and finds no consistent partisan bias.

In an analysis of 95 Senate elections, Adam Schiffer found that factors like incumbency, finances, poll standing, competitiveness, the state of the economy, and scandals explain the bulk of variation. But he did find a remaining slight advantage for Democrats in newspaper tone, even accounting for these factors.

Even where careful researchers do find bias, they tend not to find that it favors the same party all the time. Kim Fridkin Kahn and Patrick Kenney examined the positive or negative tone of each article and its coverage of issues and candidate traits and counted the number of criticisms of each candidate. They found that newspaper coverage favors incumbent candidates that the newspaper endorsed on its editorial page. But systematic studies of this kind depend on research choices that affect the results. If one candidate is quoted attacking another candidate, that shows up as a criticism, but it could reflect either an accurate portrayal of the opposing candidate's message or a choice by the reporter to emphasize the criticism. If a reporter mentions that one candidate has raised more money than another, it reflects both a reality about the race and a choice to mention fundraising over another indicator of support.

One might think that cataloging only the clearest instances of media bias is a solution to this problem, but media bias could be subtle. One study found, for example, that candidates endorsed by a newspaper get better-looking photographs in that newspaper.

The most famous study of media bias, by Tim Groseclose and Jeffrey Milyo, compared citations of interest groups and think tanks by media outlets with citations by members of Congress. They reasoned that an unbiased media outlet would cite material equally from sources favored by legislators in each party and from each ideological perspective. They found that most media outlets disproportionately cited sources favored by Democratic and more liberal members. Their measure of media bias allowed them to compare media outlets with members of Congress on the same ideological dimension.

But another study found that Groseclose and Milyo's methodology did not produce stable estimates over time. All outlets they studied appeared to be more moderate or conservative in later years. Brendan Nyhan leveled a different critique of Groseclose and Milyo: Democratic office holders and media organizations both cited more neutral experts, rather than favoring liberal perspectives: "Technocratic centrist to liberal organizations like Brookings and the Center on Budget and Policy Priorities tend to have more credentialed experts with peer-reviewed publications than their conservative counterparts." But conservatives also tend to doubt the ability of academic experts to maintain neutrality for the same reason that they are skeptical of the media: academics are also disproportionately Democrats and liberals. So the media bias debate reflects a broader conflict over whether technocratic expertise can be seen as neutral.

Despite these difficulties, studies of the relative treatment of Democratic and Republican candidates and their affiliated interest groups are relatively easy to conduct because there is a straightforward comparative baseline: balanced coverage of each candidate or each group. But that means the focus has been mostly on partisan biases, especially in election coverage, rather than broader ideological biases in the selection or description of political issues and events.

It may be easier, however, for reporters to treat two general election candidates or two parties in a congressional debate equally than it is to avoid ideological influences on coverage that stem from the reporters' underlying values. There is no evidence of a reporters' conspiracy to help the Democrats, but reporters with liberal viewpoints might (even inadvertently) choose different news to cover or frame it differently than does the much smaller number of conservative reporters.

The Promise of New Measures of Media Bias

State-of-the-art measures of media bias build on Groseclose and Milyo's strategy of comparing media outlets with members of Congress, but use "big data" approaches geared toward analyzing large sets of texts. This approach tries to capture more subtle biases in the use of language or the discussion of issues, which it might be more difficult for reporters to control.

In 2010, Matthew Gentzkow and Jesse Shapiro used the full 2005 Congressional Record to generate phrases disproportionately used by more liberal or conservative members of Congress and then compare the usage of those phrases across newspapers. This approach sidesteps some of the objections to Groseclose and Milyo's methodology by going beyond group citations, but it is still dependent on the idea that liberal and conservative legislators both use equivalently biased phrases and that, to be unbiased, reporters should tend to use them in roughly equal measure.

The approach still raises perennial difficulties in interpretation. The phrases disproportionately used by Democrats, according to Grentzkow and Shapiro, include some partisan messaging tropes—such as "workers' rights," "nuclear option," "sniper rifles," and "privatize Social Security"—but also nonpartisan, generic terms such as "trade agreement," "American people," "budget deficit," and "war in Iraq." Other Democratic phrases, such as "veterans' health care," "Congressional Black Caucus," and "minimum wage" reflect real partisan differences, but these are differences in issue agenda rather than message. Republican phrases similarly include poll-tested partisan language such as "death tax," "illegal aliens," "oil for food scandal," and "personal retirement accounts," but also neutral language referring to the names of courts and justices. Again, there are phrases that reflect issue priorities but not biased analysis, such as "stem cell" and "government spending." When reporters use these phrases, it may reflect anything from the neutral language in a paper's style guide to biased choices of what issues to cover to unfairly repeating one side's message more often. It is also difficult to distinguish between a reporter echoing liberal or conservative talking points and one side just being more "on message" in their communications with reporters.

Gregory Martin and Ali Yurukoglu recently used the same method to look for biased phrase usage on CNN, Fox News, and MSNBC in 2000, 2004, and 2008. They turned up significant but unsurprising Republican bias on Fox News and Democratic bias on MSNBC. Yet once again, the word lists found to be biased (based on congressional communications) alternatively instill confidence and raise questions. The most "Democratic" phrases included neutral language like "African American," "Republican leadership," and "Bush administration," along with more partisan phrases like "social justice" and "working families." The most "Republican" phrases included neutral phrases like "federal government" and "new refinery," alongside such ideologically tinged language as "death tax," "illegal aliens," and "limited government."

In a thoughtful appendix, the authors use several alternative measures to find similar trends. They analyze each year independently and all years together, they use different estimators of ideological position based on the same texts, and they produce an alternative measure: the time given to Democratic and Republican guests on each network. All measures produce the same basic contrast: Fox News is to the right of CNN and MSNBC and Fox

News and MSNBC are getting more polarized over time. There is no reason to doubt these basic findings.

The improvement in measurement is quite welcome. But scholars should not lose sight of qualitative differences among media outlets. Regardless of word usage patterns, we should still categorically distinguish between CNN, which goes out of its way to find balanced panels of commentators even if it does not always succeed, and Fox and MSNBC. Similarly, we should be able to separate the journalism displayed on such Fox programs as Special Report with Bret Baier and Fox News Sunday from clearly biased programming such as the Sean Hannity Show. Even if the front page of a nonpartisan newspaper is subtly biased, this is qualitatively different from the bias openly displayed on the editorial page. Losing sight of that difference downplays the change wrought by the rise of openly partisan and ideological media.

Clever Ways to Study Media Bias

Assuming that scholars can measure the relative ideological position of news organizations, it is still more difficult to locate the zero point of unbiased news. As Tim Groeling has pointed out, we do not know the population of real-world events that might neutrally be covered, so it is hard to tell if news judgment is biased or reflects neutrality. Does Trump receive negative coverage because the press hates him, or because he has produced a lot of detrimental news for himself?

Several recent studies of media bias use clever methods to get around these difficulties, but do not find consistent results. One study used an experiment where similar letters to the editor favoring each presidential candidate were sent to different newspapers. The researchers, perhaps surprisingly, found that newspapers were more likely to publish the letter against the candidate that it had endorsed, possibly as a way of balancing the opinion section. But the judgment of the editors may not correspond to the choices of that newspaper's reporters.

Another useful method is to compare coverage of similar events. One study showed that the same level of approval ratings for different presidents was covered differently by each network, reflecting partisan biases. Another study compared the coverage of similar economic statistics in different administrations, finding that the partisan editorial stance of the newspaper was associated with more positive coverage of the same unemployment rate for the endorsed presidents, but that other economic statistics had no partisan slant. A third study used instances where members of Congress switch political parties to look at changes in coverage for the same members in different parties. It found no significant party differences.

Another difficulty is that even biased coverage could reflect the media outlet's perception of its audience's views, rather than its own biases. One useful study found biased newspaper coverage of unemployment based on the party holding the White House, but found that this bias was substantially moderated after a competing newspaper closed. Apparently the newspapers took partisan approaches primarily to distinguish themselves from the other paper in town.

Perceptions of Bias Are Reducing Trust in News and Empowering Partisan Media

Regardless of the academic research, the public, and political professionals, are responding to their own perceptions of bias. William Eveland and Dhavan Shah found that even when Republicans and Democrats watch the same coverage, Democrats believe that it is more favorable for the Republican candidates and vice versa. Another study found that even presenting the same information but varying the label of where it came from (CNN or Fox) also changes the perceptions of bias.

Not surprisingly, then, faith in the news media has been in decline across the board. Yet mainstream media outlets get especially poor trust ratings from conservatives. Because

Republicans regularly cite political bias in the mainstream media, their electorate only trusts explicitly conservative alternatives.

Given the strength of partisanship in contemporary political life, it is understandable that Republicans would be more likely to suspect and react to perceived biases among (disproportionately liberal) reporters. It would be surprising if the political views of reporters did not in any way affect their selection of news stories or their portrayal of events.

Only two out of the hundred largest newspapers endorsed Trump in 2016, so there is no reason to believe that perceptions of bias will be diminishing any time soon. Trump's constant attacks on the media and invocations of "fake news" mean that the Republican electorate is likely to further reduce its trust in mainstream media and rely even more on explicitly conservative media. Fox News and talk radio have large effects on their audiences, and even on the friends of viewers and listeners who do not themselves watch or listen. They have also changed the behavior of legislators, instilling fears of primary challenges and base backlashes.

Even if Republican skepticism of mainstream media impartiality is justified, the rise of explicitly ideological media as the central information sources for Republicans is still alarming. It is as if Republicans reacted to perceived biases on the front page of the *New York Times* by deciding to only read the editorial page of the *Wall Street Journal*.

The die may therefore be cast for increasingly replacing traditional journalism with partisan media. Even as Democrats are more accepting of the mainstream news media, the recent doubling of MSNBC viewership suggests that liberals may eventually succeed at copying the conservative media model. The dominance of independent, trusted, putatively impartial media is not a natural state of affairs. It is a twentieth-century phenomenon that is not guaranteed to survive.

Be careful what you call biased news; complaints about mainstream journalism are empowering outlets that are not even trying to be even-handed.

15

Social Media Influences Political Polarization

Lee De-Wit, Cameron Brick, and Sander Van Der Linden

Lee De-Wit, PhD, is a lecturer in political psychology at Cambridge University. Sander Van Der Linden, PhD, is assistant professor of social psychology and director of the Cambridge Social Decision-Making Lab at the University of Cambridge. Cameron Brick, PhD, is a social psychologist and research associate at the University of Cambridge, U.K.

Americans are more politically polarized than ever. Many people blame social media for the increasing divide. In some aspects, social media may encourage polarization by allowing people to live in a filter bubble, where they interact online with people who hold similar political views. Research from Duke University suggests that being exposed to opposite political opinions on social media may also be driving polarization. Social media may also have another subtle effect that encourages polarization when it becomes news and influences political debate on traditional media platforms.

Americans are more divided along party lines than ever before. In the past two decades, the percentage of Americans who consistently hold liberal or conservative beliefs—rather than a mix of the two, which is the case for most people—has jumped

"Are Social Media Driving Political Polarization?" by Lee De-Wit, Cameron Brick, and Sander Van Der Linden, The Greater Good Science Center at the University of California, January 16, 2019. This article originally appeared on *Greater Good*, the online magazine of the Greater Good Science Center at UC Berkeley. Reprinted by permission.

from 10 percent to over 20. At the same time, beliefs about the other side are becoming more negative. Since 1994, the number of Americans who see the opposing political party as a threat to "the nation's well-being" has doubled. This deepening polarization has predictable results: government shutdowns, violent protests, and scathing attacks on elected officials.

Why are we becoming more polarized?

There are probably many reasons. Could social media be driving polarization? Many people think so—and, indeed, Facebook, Reddit, and Twitter have all become sites of ferocious political argument. While polarization definitely plays out on social media, the evidence to date suggests that its impact is subtler than you might think. Social media, it seems, amp up moral and emotional messages while organizing people into digital communities based on tribal conflicts.

This makes consensus building more difficult—but, as we'll discuss, it could also pave a more cooperative path forward.

Do We Live in "Filter Bubbles"?

Many people argue that we increasingly live in online filter bubbles that only expose us to the ideas we already agree with. This is consistent with a broader psychological literature on confirmation bias, showing that we are more likely to seek out and agree with views that align with our pre-existing beliefs. Selecting our preferred news sites and curating our social media accounts potentially makes it easier to listen to groups or individuals who validate our own worldviews.

The filter bubble idea has recently been elegantly demonstrated in the lab by Cass Sunstein and Tali Sharot and colleagues. The authors tested who participants would turn to for advice in categorizing geometric shapes—an obviously non-political task. In fact, this study found, participants preferred to seek advice from people who held similar political views, deciding that they must be more competent—despite evidence to the contrary!

If following people on social media who are more aligned with your worldview exacerbates polarization, then it follows that listening to "the other side" would reduce polarization. However, a recent experiment found essentially the opposite.

Christopher Bail and colleagues from Duke University recruited hundreds of Democrats and Republicans who were active on Twitter, and paid them to follow a Twitter bot that would retweet content from the opposing side. After a month of exposure, the Democrats retained about the same attitudes—but the Republicans ended up more conservative than when they started the study! This result suggests that polarization in the US could be driven by exposure to views people disagree with, rather than being separated from them by filter bubbles.

There are several ways of interpreting this result. For example, it could be that participants were reacting directly to the content of the messages they were exposed to on Twitter, but it could also be the case that they were simply responding to the messengers, not the message. In other words, the issues are not as important as group affiliation. Whatever the interpretation, this study suggests that more work is required to understand to what extent filter bubbles might drive political polarization.

A study by Levi Boxell and colleagues provided a simpler test of the role of the Internet: Is more social media use associated with more polarization? Boxell and colleagues assessed polarization in the US for different age ranges—and they surprisingly found that polarization was highest for the age groups that use the Internet and social media the least, such as older adults (75+).

This suggests that if the Internet is fueling polarization, its influence might be more indirect. This indirect influence is plausible, however, because in many traditional newsrooms, activity on social media has itself become news. Indeed, Trump has proved particularly successful in dominating the traditional news media (TV and print) with his activity on Twitter.

Thus, it is possible that the climate of debate on social media influences the tone of debate on other media platforms. Could social media influence polarization even in Americans who rely on the traditional media?

How Social Media Shape Debate

William Brady and colleagues tested what types of political messages on Twitter are more likely to be shared. When the researchers looked at tweets from the Presidential, Senate, and House of Representatives candidates in the 2016 US election, they found that tweets with more emotive and moral words were more likely to be retweeted. All voters responded more to words showing moral outrage, but effects were somewhat stronger for tweets from Republican candidates, and Republicans were more likely to respond to emotional words about patriotism or religion.

This work suggests that if politicians want to maximize their impact on Twitter, they need to resort to more moral and emotive vocabulary. This in turn might help explain why encouraging people to follow politicians from the opposing side appears to worsen polarization: Politicians tweet the policy positions that their political base wants to hear, of course—but they do so in moral and emotive language that may create negative reactions from the opposing side.

This language itself becomes news, as reporters turn tweets into headlines that can generate fear on the "other side." In this way, the whole news cycle shifts towards more polarizing and emotionally laden content.

According to Gordon Allport's "contact hypothesis," contact between groups lessens prejudice. However, decades of research testing this hypothesis has found some limitations. Although intergroup contact does tend to increase cooperation—and reduce prejudice—the positive effect may depend on important contextual factors, such as the nature of the conflict and whether the groups have equal status or a common goal. As Allport put it, sometimes more contact can lead to more trouble. That appears to be the case on Twitter.

Can We Build Social-Media Bridges?

So, perhaps we need to start thinking about how to structure interactions between groups on social media so that conflict becomes less likely and cooperation becomes more possible.

Social media companies need to do more themselves to counter online extremism and polarization by, for example, better regulating the political targeting of ads on their platforms. However, even in the absence of change in policy or on the sites themselves, there is a lot we can do as individuals to make social media less polarized.

A distinctive feature of social media is the importance of social consensus cues or online endorsement (e.g., likes, shares). Some research shows that the presence of these distinctive social cues can actually trigger decisions to select news in a way that reduces selective political exposure. In other words, if a story has been upvoted or shared a million times, it is likely to burst your bubble, even when the content is not ideologically congenial.

We can also try to cultivate a diverse network, extending beyond our immediate circles. It's not necessarily a good thing that social media increase the volume of information that we receive from people whom we already know well. Rather, research suggests that even when we are not exposed to the "other side" directly, so-called "weak ties" (friends of friends, acquaintances) offer a degree of political diversity that might inspire more political moderation.

Unfortunately, as the research we've discussed suggests, this diversity won't necessarily lead to harmony, since you're more likely to encounter strong emotional and moral language that could trigger negative partisan reactions. You might find the antidote in a trait known as Actively Open-Minded Thinking (AOT). AOT is a cognitive style that allows people to be more thoughtful, flexible, and open-minded, even when information contradicts a strongly held prior view. For example, both conservatives and liberals who score higher in AOT are less likely to display strong polarization on hot-button issues, such as climate change. Similarly, a new study earlier this year found that high-AOT Twitter users were better at creating and responding to social media content in a thoughtful and reflective manner.

In short, perhaps the solution to our problem is not completely out of reach. When we treat online spaces like we would treat our own community, difficult conversations become more productive. No matter how confident in our arguments or aggrieved we feel, everyone benefits when we actively try to be more thoughtful and open-minded about what we say—and how we react to others with whom we disagree—both online and offline.

16

Journalists Should Spend Less Time on Twitter

John P. Wihbey

John P. Wihbey is an assistant professor of journalism and media innovation at Northeastern University, where he heads the graduate programs in the School of Journalism.

Is the news media partisan? That might depend on the outlet for which they work. However, in general, journalists' increasing reliance on Twitter could be partly to blame for any partisanship occurring in journalism today. There is reason to be concerned about such polarization worsening over time. Another way to avoid bias is for journalists to be better trained in data analysis. Competency in interpreting research and data will help reporters see through bias coming from their sources.

You hear a lot of heated claims and baseless generalities these days about what's wrong with the news media.

What's seldom heard is what the underlying data indicate about true problem areas and where journalists need to improve.

News reporting requires doing a lot of things well, but two crucial elements are being independent of political (or other) interests and knowing one's subject well enough to select what's important for the public.

"Prescription for Journalists from Journalists: Less Time Studying Twitter, More Time Studying Math," by John P. Wihbey, The Conversation Media Group Ltd, May 1, 2019. https://theconversation.com/prescription-for-journalists-from-journalists-less-time-studying-twitter-more-time-studying-math-113248.

I am a media scholar and former journalist. In my research for my book *The Social Fact: News and Knowledge in a Networked World*, I tried to quantify certain aspects of these two dimensions of news media.

While the overall evidence shows journalists to be ethical in their practice and fair and public-spirited in their mission, I found some troubling signs in my research.

Partisanship

The first question I looked at was whether journalists were partisan. That would affect their stories by making them biased and therefore less trustworthy.

Research in general continues to show news media have left- and right-leaning partisan slants, although the degree depends on the outlet and subject in question.

But one novel aspect to consider in our hyper-polarized, social media-driven age is the relationship between journalists' work and their online social networks, in particular Twitter, where reporters and editors spend a lot of time these days.

Is partisanship visible not just in the reporting of stories, but elsewhere, in the social networks that journalists inhabit?

As part of a 2018 study with my colleagues Kenny Joseph of the University at Buffalo, SUNY, and David Lazer at Northeastern University, we analyzed partisanship across more than 300,000 news articles produced by 644 journalists at 25 different US news outlets.

We did this using algorithms that helped us sort and analyze each article and journalist, from more conservative outlets such as the *Wall Street Journal* and *National Review* to more liberal ones such as the *New Yorker* and the *New York Times*.

We looked at the frequency with which key political terms were used, such as "LGBT," "equal pay," and "Voting Rights Act" for left-leaning persons, and "bureaucrats," "illegal immigrants" and "sponsor of terrorism" for right-leaning persons.

We then compared this analysis with a careful look at the individual journalists' social networks on Twitter—which accounts they follow, and the degree of partisanship of these accounts.

Twitter is a figurative water cooler where journalists spend hours, and surely it shapes some of what they believe is important and colors their views. Research suggests that journalists see Twitter as valuable for their work, and they use the platform at relatively high rates compared to the public at large. We did not design our research to be able to establish true causation, but rather set out to explore just how much of a correlation there was.

Overall, what we found was a modest correlation between the partisanship of the personal network a journalist follows on Twitter and the content she produces. Of course, just because a journalist chooses to follow, say, mostly conservative social media accounts doesn't mean she will necessarily skew her journalism in that direction. It is not a mechanical relationship. But the data show a reasonably strong connection.

There is solid evidence of partisan segregation stretching across the news and social media worlds, and society should be worried about trends that might make polarization worse over time.

Competence

The second issue to consider in terms of areas of improvement for journalism is the degree to which journalists may not have sufficient knowledge or understanding of certain issues in order to inform the public properly.

Even if President Donald Trump's criticism of the media is usually bombastic and misguided, it's certainly legitimate to inquire about the competence and knowledge of news outlets.

We have been asking reporters and editors both about their knowledge and skills and their aspirations for the profession in survey work we are conducting through the Shorenstein Center on Media, Politics, and Public Policy at Harvard.

It's clear there are many journalists who have substantial knowledge of many public affairs topics. But the profession continues to struggle with competence in a variety of areas, particularly with reporting about numbers, data and research.

Across the board, journalists know they should be better able to do quantitative analysis and interpret information more critically, a finding in our survey research. They know these skills are key to seeing through the potential bias of sources, be they politicians, health care companies, energy firms, Wall Street, Madison Avenue or the White House.

For example, when a police department makes a claim about reducing crime, or a health care provider touts progress on patient safety, skeptical journalists with good data skills will have greater ability to analyze the data themselves, see through faulty claims and call out misinformation.

Yet the training and preparation for the profession of journalism often falls short. As a journalism educator myself, I fully admit that the responsibility and burden are very much on us, as educators, to provide training in these areas, particularly as the world grows more complex and data-driven.

Taking a hard look at the press is not easy at this time, as it can seem to feed the lies about journalism fueled by the president. All of this analysis is not to validate the often poisonous criticisms of the press in recent years, which have tended toward exaggeration.

But if we are to have any hope of regaining broad public trust in professional news media—and improve public knowledge and discourse in the way that most people want—we need to start by getting much more empirical about what is wrong and what is right with our media institutions.

17

As Gerrymandering Rises, Political Polarization Increases

John Rennie Short

John Rennie Short is a professor of geography and public policy in the School of Public Policy at the University of Maryland, Baltimore County. He is an expert on urban issues, environmental concerns, globalization, political geography, and the history of cartography.

Gerrymandering, the practice of manipulating a voting district's legislative boundaries to favor a political party, is on the rise. The practice of gerrymandering has increased in recent decades as party officials have realized how effective gerrymandering can be to hold power in the US House of Representatives. With sophisticated computer programs and detailed voter information, political parties can precisely adjust voting boundaries to yield the highest benefit. To date, the US Supreme Court has declined to intervene in legal cases involving gerrymandering. With little consensus on a solution, gerrymandering will continue to impact US elections and America's political polarization.

"4 Reasons Gerrymandering Is Getting Worse," by John Rennie Short, The Conversation Media Group Ltd, October 29, 2018. https://theconversation.com/4-reasons-gerrymandering-is-getting-worse-105182.

November's midterm elections are some of the most eagerly awaited, closely watched and hyperpartisan for many years.

But the results for many congressional House seats are already known because the election will occur at a time of rampant gerrymandering.

For example, Maryland's 3rd Congressional District is drawn up in a way that guarantees the 2018 election victory of Democratic incumbent John Sarbanes. Congressional districts in Texas are drawn up to favor Republicans, such as Mike Conway, who is assured victory in the 11th District.

The mechanism is simple: The political party that controls state legislatures gets to redraw congressional boundaries every 10 years after the results of the most recent Census. Gerrymandering is the partisan redrawing of these boundaries. Basically, it allows politicians to select their voters rather than the voters to choose their representatives.

In 2012, Republicans won a majority of 33 seats in the House despite getting 1.4 million fewer votes than their Democratic opponents. In the past four congressional elections, Republicans have won a larger share of seats than their share of nationwide votes. These results are a sure sign that gerrymandering is involved.

The term "gerrymandering" originates with the activities of Elbridge Gerry, who in 1810 as governor of Massachusetts signed a bill that created legislative boundaries that favored his political party. A cartoonist of the day depicted the boundaries as a salamander. The system was so "gerrymandered" that the Democratic-Republicans won only 49 percent of the votes but picked up 72 percent of the seats.

Gerrymandering involves what's called the "cracking and packing" of voters by moving the boundaries of voting districts. Cracking spreads opposition voters thinly across many districts to dilute their power. Packing concentrates opposition voters in fewer districts to reduce the number of seats they can win.

There are four main reasons why gerrymandering has gotten worse in the last 20 years.

1. It Makes a Difference

First, gerrymandering is effective in helping political parties hold power in the House.

Since 1995, after 40 years of uninterrupted Democratic dominance, the House has become more competitive because in large part the South turned Republican.

As the Dixie Democratic stronghold became a Republican bastion, the House came into play. Republicans took control from 1995 to 2007, Democrats won back the house in 2007 and Republicans regained control in 2011. Gerrymandering is now seen as a way to tip the scales in a more competitive climate.

One political consultant, Thomas Hofeller, described by many as a gerrymander genius, was particularly effective in designing redistricting strategies for Republicans between 1992 and 2017. He was one of the first to realize that redrawing boundaries was one way to elect as many Republicans as possible. In 1992 he worked for the Republican National Committee in drawing congressional maps in Arizona, Michigan, Minnesota and Ohio. He subsequently advised Republican politicians across the country on how to redraw electoral maps to their advantage.

2. More Effective Technology

Second, gerrymandering has become a much more effective tool in the last 20 years. With sophisticated computer programs and ever more detailed information on voters' location and preferences, politicians can now crack and pack with surgical precision.

Maryland's 3rd Congressional District slithers and slides across the state to pick up as many Democratic voters as possible. A Republican Texas packs Democratic voters into a few seats to ensure a Republican majority. With pinpoint accuracy afforded by these new technologies, state legislatures are able to ensure victory for their party.

3. The Supreme Court

The third reason is that the Supreme Court has effectively sanctioned gerrymandering.

In 1986, the court in *Thornburg v. Gingles* ruled against a Democratic legislature's attempt to thinly spread minority voters among seven new districts in North Carolina. The case was brought by minority groups in the state who felt it impaired their ability to elect representatives of their choice in violation of the Voting Rights Act of 1965. The ruling helped create districts where minority voters were concentrated, so-called majority-minority seats, and hence encouraged the future packing of voters.

When the Republican-controlled Pennsylvania legislature proposed a partisan redistricting plan after the 2000 Census, members of the Democratic Party sued in federal court that it was unconstitutional under the one-person, one-vote principle of Article 1, Section 2 of the Constitution. In *Vieth v. Jubelirer* in 2004, the court ruled 5-4 not to intervene. Predictably, partisan gerrymandering then increased especially after the redistricting round after the 2010 Census.

Shelby County Alabama filed a case against the constitutionality of the 1965 Voting Rights Act that protected voters' rights in the South. In *Shelby v. Holder* in 2013, the court in a 5-4 ruling overturned key elements of the act. The ruling encouraged partisan gerrymandering in areas of the country previously under federal scrutiny.

In 2017, and again in 2018, the Supreme Court passed up numerous opportunities to decide upon the constitutional legality or illegality of gerrymandering. The Supreme Court's choice not to intervene has emboldened ever more partisan gerrymandering.

4. No Likely Solution

A fourth reason is that it is difficult for the courts to agree on solutions. There are numerous potential solutions. The efficiency gap for example measures the number of "wasted" votes for a party that cannot win in a district. The difference between the wasted votes for each side, divided by the total number of votes, is the efficiency gap. It was used to assess the Republican 2011 redistricting plan in Wisconsin.

But technical problems remain in dealing with the complexity of creating fair elections under the "winner take all" system we currently have.

So, some people argue for a major overhaul of our electoral system to overcome gerrymandering. For example, under equal weighting, voters rank candidates in order of preference rather than just choosing one. Proportional representation would involve major changes to our current electoral system and is unlikely in the near future.

Polarized Politics

Gerrymandering has a pernicious impact on the electoral system and on the wider democratic process. It encourages long-term incumbency and a consequent polarization of political discourses. In gerrymandered districts, politicians only need to appeal to their base rather than to a wider electorate.

Legal challenges to gerrymandering may succeed, but until then it remains an ugly fact of the US electoral system that belies our claim to be a democracy. The results of the upcoming election will reflect the redistricting designs of politicians as much as the will of the people.

18

Ideological Differences, Not Gerrymandering, Are Driving Political Polarization

Harry J. Enten

Harry J. Enten is a senior writer and analyst for CNN Politics, where he specializes in data-driven journalism and covers politics with a focus on poll numbers and electoral trends.

Gerrymandering is not the leading cause of rising political polarization across America. Instead, natural geographic divisions at both the state and local level—with Democrats more likely to live in urban areas and Republicans in suburban and rural regions—play a significant role in growing political polarization. Additionally, increasing ideological differences between Democrats and Republicans make it more difficult for legislators to come together in Congress.

You ever hear a point of view that is so infuriating that you want to stick your head out the window and yell? I go bananas when I hear an opinion that goes against well-established political science literature.

That happened this past weekend when respected television journalist Tom Brokaw said the House of Representatives is becoming increasingly polarized because of *gerrymandering*.

"Why 'Gerrymandering' Doesn't Polarise Congress the Way We're Told," by Harry J. Enten, Guardian News & Media Limited, January 3, 2013. Reprinted by permission.

Don't get me wrong, I love Brokaw. It just so happens that he is wrong, and posts about the effect of gerrymandering on redistricting have been written over and over again in past months.

It could be that Brokaw doesn't quite understand what gerrymandering is. For those who don't, gerrymandering is the manipulation in the drawing of House districts to ensure a desired result. Brokaw's assumption is that politics is becoming more polarized as the result of gerrymandering in districts in which Democrats and Republicans are increasingly safe from worrying about a competitive challenger from the other party.

While it is true that House districts are increasingly "safe," this is the case even when controlling for redistricting. Last week, Nate Silver noted that there was an 8% increase in polarization independent of any effects of redistricting in 2012.

Much of this change is because states themselves are becoming more polarized. As I pointed out in my last article, the number of swing states in presidential elections is at an all-time low. The number of Democratic and Republican senators from states that lean Democratic and Republican on the presidential level respectively is way up. Partially as a result, there is an increasingly large gap in ideology between Democratic and Republican senators, which has tracked with the ideological gap in the House. So unless we are, all of a sudden, redistricting state lines, then gerrymandering can't possibly be the cause of what we're seeing at the state level.

Part of what's going on in the House is that there is a natural inclination for Democrats to crowd into cities and Republicans to spread themselves out in suburban and rural areas. In New York City alone, there were five Democratic members of Congress re-elected with at least 90% of the vote. Jowei Chen and Jonathan Rodden ran redistricting simulations on the precinct level and still ran up against a natural bias that prevents Democrats being able to win more seats because of their urban concentrations. There really isn't any way to fix this issue—at least, not by redistricting.

Nolan McCarty, Keith Poole, and Howard Rosenthal computerized redistricting with the aim of creating "fair" non-gerrymandered districts. Even when they tried their best to have "many heterogeneous and competitive districts," the predicted level of polarization didn't differ much from what we have today. Keep in mind, of course, that this sort of redistricting also would reduce the number of minority members of Congress because it neglects the Voting Rights Act. I get the feeling that wouldn't be particularly popular.

We see this in Nicholas Goedert examination of the 2012 House results, too. Goedert looked at seats in which redistricting was controlled by Democrats, by Republicans, by bipartisan committees or by courts. Controlling for past-vote-to-seat curves, Goedert determined that when redistricting was nonpartisan or bipartisan, Democrats underperformed by an average of 7 pt (that is, they only take 50% of seats when projected to get 57%).

This is absolutely key. Fair redistricting just doesn't have the impact you might think. Once we control for incumbency, Democrats are at an inherent disadvantage that dates back to the 1950s—long before Republicans controlled a majority of the redistricting processes.

Speaking of the effect of incumbency (that is, incumbents run ahead of what the national House vote would indicate), you'll notice that it had a major effect the last few cycles. According to Think Progress, Democrats would have needed to have taken the national House vote by 7 pt in 2012 to have won a majority of seats. The author, Ian Millhiser, blames this on gerrymandering.

Here's the problem. After the 2008 House election, which was fought under Republican-gerrymandered district lines of 2000 district lines seats, the Democrats, who were already the majority party in the House, actually controlled more seats than they should have—given a 10.5 pt victory in the national House vote.

The vote-to-seat curve will likely bounce closer to equal when incumbent Republicans sense a wave and retire, as they did in 2008.

None of this is to say that partisan gerrymandering doesn't have any effect. Sam Wang believes Republicans are far more likely to gain seats than Democrats when they control the redistricting process. Goedert's analysis, which includes more states, agrees, but also shows that Democrats are likely to take more seats than they should if they gerrymander as well. Goedert demonstrates that Republicans gain more seats by about 18 percentage points in a state when they control redistricting. Democrats pick up only about 9 pt more when they draw the lines. This difference is, in my opinion, likely a reflection of the natural disadvantage Democrats have in redistricting—as seen in the 7 pt Democratic underperformance in the non- and bipartisan states.

Overall, even if all the states redid their lines under "fair" rules, and given the Democratic win by 1 pt in the 2012 House popular vote, Republicans would likely still maintain about 225 seats in the new Congress.

To correct for this imbalance, *you would have to gerrymander*. That is, you would have to manipulate the drawing of House districts to ensure the desired result. You'd need to have weird lines that snake from neighborhood to neighborhood, ignoring geographical integrity. That's not only against the law in many states, it would also make congressmen and women unrepresentative of at least part of their long, winding districts.

Yet, this doesn't tell the entire story. All of this analysis is based on the idea that the partisanship of the district causes the partisanship of the legislator. However, the difference in ideology between Republicans and Democrats in competitive districts and Republicans and Democrats in uncompetitive districts respectively is actually relatively small.

The real difference is how Republicans and Democrats differ ideologically in similarly partisan districts. McCarty and Boris Shor found that even in 50/50 districts (that is, those split evenly between Democrats and Republicans), the ideological divergence between Democratic and Republican representatives has climbed much higher in the past 40 years. So, even if you were to gerrymander evenly competitive districts, you would not likely see everyone coming together in Congress.

Anyway you put it, Democrat and Republican legislators have greater ideological differences than ever. Gerrymandering probably doesn't help, yet it's not the major cause of the problem. Natural geographic divisions on the state and local level between Democrats and Republicans are a big cause in this growing polarization. Both of these, though, fail to account for the fact that even when controlling for district partisanship, there are increasing ideological differences between Democrats and Republicans in Congress.

Organizations to Contact

The editors have compiled the following list of organizations concerned with the issues debated in this book. The descriptions are derived from materials provided by the organizations. All have publications or information available for interested readers. The list was compiled on the date of publication of the present volume; the information provided here may change. Be aware that many organizations take several weeks or longer to respond to inquiries, so allow as much time as possible.

American Enterprise Institute for Public Policy Research (AEI)

1789 Massachusetts Avenue NW, Washington, DC 20036
(202) 862-5800
website: www.aei.org

AEI is a conservative research and education organization that studies national and international issues and conducts political and public opinion studies. AEI scholars and staff strive to deliver content that supports freedom, increasing individual opportunities and strengthening free enterprise. The institute has numerous publications, including reports, journals, monthly periodicals, working papers, and books.

Bipartisan Policy Center

1225 Eye Street NW, Suite 1000, Washington, DC 20005
(202) 204-2400
email: bipartisaninfo@bipartisanpolicy.org
website: www.bipartisanpolicy.org

The Bipartisan Policy Center is a think tank dedicated to fostering bipartisanship in the United States by combining the best ideas from both Democratic and Republicans for Americans' health, security, and opportunity. The center's website provides information about a variety of policy areas, press releases, news articles and reports, and local events.

Brookings Institution

1775 Massachusetts Avenue NW, Washington, DC 20036
(202) 797-6000
email: communications@brookings.edu
website: www.brookings.edu

The Brookings Institution is a nonprofit public policy organization that conducts research on problems facing society at the local, national, and global levels. The institution's over 300 experts in government and academia provide quality research, policy recommendations, and analysis on a wide range of public policy issues.

Cato Institute

1000 Massachusetts Avenue NW, Washington, DC 20001
(202) 842-0200
website: www.cato.org

The Cato Institute is a public policy research organization that strives to support the principles of individual liberty, limited government, free markets, and peace. The institute's scholars and staff provide independent, nonpartisan research on a variety of policy issues.

Center for American Progress

1333 H Street NW, 10th Floor, Washington, DC 20005
(202) 682-1611
website: www.americanprogress.org

The Center for American Progress is a progressive policy institute that strives to improve the lives of Americans. The center's policy teams develop new ideas in major issue areas and use an extensive communications and outreach effort to promote these ideas in the national debate. The center's website provides information about a variety of issues, press releases, local events, newsletters, and more.

Democratic National Committee (DNC)

430 South Capitol Street SE, Washington, DC 20003
(202) 863-8000
website: www.democrats.org

The Democratic National Committee is the main organization that governs the Democratic Party in the United States. The committee's website includes information about the party's platform, current issues, press releases, local events and organizations, and more.

Heritage Foundation

214 Massachusetts Avenue NE, Washington, DC 20002
(202) 546-4400
email: info@heritage.org
website: www.heritage.org

The Heritage Foundation is a conservative public policy research organization that strives to promote conservative public policies that support the principles of free enterprise, limited government, and individual freedom. The foundation's staff performs research on policy issues and presents their findings to government policy makers and legislators, the news media, and other academic and policy communities.

Pew Research Center

1615 L Street NW, Suite 800, Washington, DC 20036
(202) 419-4300
email: info@pewresearch.org
website: www.pewresearch.org

The Pew Research Center is a nonpartisan fact tank that provides information to the general public about the issues, attitudes, and trends affecting society. The center's analysts conduct public opinion polling, demographic research, content analysis, and other social science research. The center's website contains information about issues, research, publications, news releases, and more.

RAND Corporation

1776 Main Street, Santa Monica, CA 90401
(310) 393-0411
email: media@rand.org
website: www.rand.org

The RAND Corporation is a nonprofit, nonpartisan research organization that strives to use research and analysis to improve policy and decision making. RAND experts and analysts conduct research across a wide variety of issues, including democracy, politics, and government.

Republican National Committee

310 First Street, Washington, DC 20003
(202) 863-8500
email: info@gop.com
website: www.gop.com

The Republican National Committee is the main organization that governs the Republican Party in the United States. The committee's website includes information about the party's platform, current issues, press releases, local events and organizations, and more.

Unite America

1580 Lincoln Street, Suite 520, Denver, CO 80203
(720) 592-0843
email: hello@uniteamerica.org
website: www.uniteamerica.org

Unite America is an organization of Democrats, Republicans, and independents whose mission is to bridge the growing partisan divide in the United States. The group strives to build a more representative and functional government by investing in nonpartisan electoral reform campaigns and electing candidates with bipartisan values.

Bibliography

Books

Jason Altmire. *Dead Center: How Political Polarization Divided America and What We Can Do About It*. Boiling Springs, PA: Sunbury Press, 2017.

Ross K. Baker. *Is Bipartisanship Dead? A Report from the Senate*. London, UK: Routledge, 2014.

A. Bennett. *Battle for the White House from Bush to Obama: Nominations and Elections in an Era of Partisanship*. London, UK: Palgrave Macmillan, 2015.

Ronald Brownstein. *The Second Civil War: How Extreme Partisanship Has Paralyzed Washington and Polarized America*. New York, NY: The Penguin Press, 2008.

Thomas Carothers and Andrew O'Donohue. *Democracies Divided: The Global Challenge of Political Polarization*. Washington, DC: Brookings Institution Press, 2019.

William F. Connelly Jr. *James Madison Rules America: The Constitutional Origins of Congressional Partisanship*. Lanham, MD: Rowman & Littlefield, 2010.

William F. Connelly Jr., John J. Pitney Jr., and Gary J. Schmitt. *Is Congress Broken? The Virtues and Defects of Partisanship and Gridlock*. Washington, DC: Brookings Institution Press, 2017.

Joanne B. Freeman. *The Field of Blood: Violence in Congress and the Road to Civil War*. New York, NY: Picador, 2018.

Mark Gerzon. *The Reunited States of America: How We Can Bridge the Partisan Divide*. Williston, VT: Berrett-Koehler Publishers, 2016.

Matthew Henry. *Working Together: Why We Need Bipartisanship in American Politics*. Potomac, MD: New Degree Press, 2018.

Nathan Kalmoe. *With Ballots and Bullets*. Cambridge, UK: Cambridge University Press, 2020.

Ezra Klein. *Why We're Polarized*. New York, NY: Simon & Schuster, 2020.

Steve Kornacki. *The Red and the Blue: The 1990s and the Birth of Political Tribalism*. New York, NY: HarperCollins, 2018.

John A. Lawrence. *Class of '74: Congress after Watergate and the Roots of Partisanship*. Baltimore, MD: Johns Hopkins University Press, 2018.

Nolan McCarty. *Polarization: What Everyone Needs to Know*. New York, NY: Oxford University Press, 2019.

Nicole Mellow. *The State of Disunion: Regional Sources of Modern American Partisanship*. Baltimore, MD: Johns Hopkins University Press, 2008.

Nathaniel Persily. *Solutions to Political Polarization in America*. New York, NY: Cambridge University Press, 2015.

John Sides and Daniel J. Hopkins. *Political Polarization in American Politics*. New York, NY: Bloomsbury, 2015.

James A. Thurber. *American Gridlock: The Sources, Character, and Impact of Political Polarization*. New York, NY: Cambridge University Press, 2016.

James I. Wallner. *Death of Deliberation: Partisanship and Polarization in the United States Senate*. Lanham, MD: Lexington Books, 2015.

Jonathan White and Lea Ypi. *The Meaning of Partisanship*. London, UK: Oxford University Press, 2016.

Periodicals and Internet Sources

Alan Abramowitz and Steven Webster, "'Negative Partisanship' Explains Everything," Politico.com, September/October 2017.

Aaron Astor, "Partisanship Is an American Tradition—and Good for Democracy," *Washington Post*, July 12, 2017.

Dan Balz, "Americans Hate All the Partisanship, but They're Also More Partisan Than They Were," *Washington Post*, October 26, 2019.

Sarah Binder, "How Political Polarization Creates Stalemate and Undermines Lawmaking," *Washington Post*, January 13, 2014.

Bipartisan Policy Center, "History of Bipartisanship." https://bipartisanpolicy.org/history-of-bipartisanship/

Fergus M. Bordewich, "'You Never Find Quiet Except Under a Tyranny.' Congress Has Always Been Partisan and That's a Good Thing," Time.com, February 21, 2020.

Thomas Carothers and Andrew O'Donohue, "How Americans Were Driven to Extremes," *Foreign Affairs*, September 25, 2019.

Jonathan Chait, "How 'Negative Partisanship' Has Transformed American Politics," *New York Magazine*, April 17, 2015.

Mike Cummings, "Study: Americans Prize Party Loyalty Over Democratic Principles," *Yale News*, August 11, 2020.

Lee Drutman, "America Is Now the Divided Republic the Framers Feared," *Atlantic*, January 2, 2020.

Lee Drutman, "Escaping the Partisan Death Spiral," *Cato Institute Policy Report*, July/August 2020.

Lee Drutman, "How Hatred Came to Dominate American Politics," FiveThirtyEight.com, October 5, 2020.

Andrew Fiala, "It's Time We Take Heed of George Washington's Warning About Partisanship," *Fresno Bee*, October 25, 2019.

Seung Min Kim, "JOBS Act Heads to Obama," Politico.com, March 27, 2012.

Evan MacDonald, "A Polarized America: How the Partisan Divide Grew Over Decades, and Why Liberals and Conservatives Just Can't Get Along," Cleveland.com, August 30, 2020.

Thomas E. Mann and Norman J. Ornstein, "Five Myths About Bipartisanship," *Washington Post*, January 17, 2020.

David A. Moss, "Fixing What's Wrong with US Politics," *Harvard Business Review*, March 2012.

Pew Research Center, "In a Politically Polarized Era, Sharp Divides in Both Partisan Coalitions," December 17, 2019.

Pew Research Center, "The Partisan Divide on Political Values Grows Even Wider," October 5, 2017.

Index

H

I

J

K

L

M

N

O

P

R

S

T

V

W

Y

Z